101
Amazing Truths
about JESUS
That You Probably Didn't Know

101

Amazing Truths about JESUS

That You Probably Didn't Know

MARK LITTLETON

HOWARD BOOKS
A DIVISION OF SIMON & SCHUSTER
New York   London   Toronto   Sydney

Our purpose at Howard Books is to:
- *Increase faith* in the hearts of growing Christians
- *Inspire holiness* in the lives of believers
- *Instill hope* in the hearts of struggling people everywhere

Because He's coming again!

 Howard Books, a division of Simon & Schuster, Inc.
HOWARD BOOKS 1230 Avenue of the Americas, New York, NY 10020

101 Amazing Truths about Jesus That You Probably Didn't Know © 2007 by Mark R. Littleton

All rights reserved, including the right to reproduce this book or portions thereof in any form whatsoever. For information, address Howard Books, 3117 North 7th Street, West Monroe, Louisiana 71291-2227

Library of Congress Cataloging-in-Publication Data is available

ISBN-13: 978-1-58229-635-7
ISBN-10:   1-58229-635-9

07 08 09 10 11 12 13 14   10 9 8 7 6 5 4 3 2 1

HOWARD is a registered trademark of Simon & Schuster, Inc.
Manufactured in United States of America
For information regarding special discounts for bulk purchases, please contact Simon & Schuster Special Sales at 1-800-456-6798 or business@simonandschuster.com.

Edited by Between the Lines
Cover design by Design Works
Interior design by John Mark Luke Designs

To *Jeanette,* my
LOYAL and LOVING
helpmate, who makes me
LAUGH when I need it
and gives me
INSIGHT and WISDOM
for the path ahead

Contents

Contents

CONTENTS

ix

Contents

CONTENTS

xi

Contents

Acknowledgments

I'd like to thank several people for their help with and confidence in this project. First of all, the editors at Howard Books have been a dream.

My wife, Jeanette, and kids—Alisha, Gardner, and Elizabeth—have all been patient with me as I worked on this book. It's been a tough journey but also a fascinating one. Thanks for your support.

I'd also like to thank Dr. John MacArthur, Dr. Charles Ryrie, and the Zondervan Corporation for their excellent study Bibles. I found them invaluable as I did the research for this book.

Finally, I thank my Father in heaven for giving me this idea and coaching me through the writing of it. He keeps making my life an adventure, and I wouldn't exchange his love and support for anything in this world.

Introduction

Jesus Christ was the most important, compelling, and transforming individual in human history. Yet many people today don't know that much about him except that he lived two thousand years ago, performed miracles, died on a cross, and then rose from the dead.

Did he really do anything that amazing?

Are there facts about him that would astonish you if you knew them?

Who was he really?

This book will reveal many of those truths. Knowing about them will not only broaden your understanding of Jesus, it will deepen your experience of him too. Be prepared for an amazing journey. Some of this information you will have heard, but some may be completely new to you. Every one of these truths, if you let them, can change your life for good. Jesus not only wants you to know *about* him; he wants you to know him personally, relationally. He came not just to redeem people from lives of sin and death but also to give them something beyond this world: himself.

I hope you enjoy the stories ahead.

101

Amazing Truths
about JESUS
That You Probably Didn't Know

1

Jesus created ALL things.

"In the beginning God created the heavens and the earth" (Genesis 1:1). For thousands of years people believed that God the Father, God Jehovah, God the self-existing one, was the Creator. But John tells us Jesus was the Creator: "Through him [Jesus] all things were made; without him nothing was made that has been made" (John 1:3).

God the Father was the architect, planner, and producer of creation. But Jesus was the agent and director, the executor of the process. This bears out in a couple of passages from other places in the New Testament. First, Colossians 1:15–17 tells us, "He [Jesus] is the image of the invisible God, the firstborn over all creation. For by him all things were created: things in heaven and on earth, visible and invisible, whether thrones or powers or rulers or authorities; all things were created by him and for him. He is before all things, and in him all things hold together."

From this we see that (1) Jesus created everything, visible and invisible; (2) everything was created "by him" and "for him"—in other words, the creation belongs to him; (3) he existed "before all things"—before anything else existed; and (4) he "holds all things together"—it is by his power that the universe does not simply explode.

Next, in Hebrews 1:2, we read: "But in these last days he has spoken to us by his Son, whom he appointed heir of all things, and through whom he made the universe." Again we see an unequivocal statement of Jesus's role as Creator.

Think about this for just a moment. When Jesus walked the earth and spoke with and healed countless people, doing miracle upon miracle, he was the one who actually had created that earth and those people. When the leading Jews insulted him and spit on him, they were mistreating the one who had fashioned them in the womb. And when people nailed him to the cross, they were in effect trying to kill the one who held their molecules and bodies together.

It's a remarkable thought. Who could possibly have understood when looking into Jesus's face and hearing his voice that they were seeing and hearing creative omnipotence?

2

Jesus's life was FORETOLD by prophecies.

Just how exact did God get in revealing the details—the who, what, where, and when—about the Messiah's coming? Let's look at a few of the prophecies.

He would be born in some special way of a woman, and he would ultimately crush the head of Satan. "I will put enmity between you [Satan] and the woman, and between your offspring and hers; he will crush your head, and you will strike his heel" (Genesis 3:15).

He would be born through Abraham. "I will make you into a great nation and I will bless you; I will make your name great, and you will be a blessing. I will bless those who bless you, and whoever curses you I will curse; and all peoples on earth will be blessed through you" (Genesis 12:2–3).

He would be born through Isaac. "The LORD appeared to Isaac and said, 'Do not go down to Egypt; live in the land where I tell you to live. Stay in this land for a while, and I will be with you and will bless you. For to you and your descendants I will give all these lands and will confirm the oath I swore to your father Abraham. I will make your descendants as numerous as the stars in the sky and will give them all these lands, and through your offspring all nations on earth will be blessed'" (Genesis 26:2–4).

He would be born through Jacob. "I am the LORD, the God of your father Abraham and the God of Isaac. I will give you and your descendants the land on which you are lying. Your descendants will be like the dust of the earth, and you will spread out to the west and to the east, to the north and to the south. All peoples on earth will be blessed through you and your offspring. I am with you and will watch over you wherever you go, and I will bring you back to this land. I will not leave you until I have done what I have promised you" (Genesis 28:13–15).

He would be born through Judah. "The scepter will not depart from Judah, nor the ruler's staff from between his feet, until he comes to whom it belongs and the obedience of the nations is his" (Genesis 49:10).

He would be born through King David. "When your days are over and you rest with your fathers, I will raise up your offspring to succeed you, who will come from your own body, and I will establish his kingdom. He is the one who will build a house for my Name, and I will establish the throne of his kingdom forever. I will be his father, and he will be my son. When he does wrong, I will punish him with the rod of men, with floggings inflicted by men. But my love will never be taken away from him, as I took it away from Saul, whom I removed from before you. Your house and your kingdom will endure forever before me; your throne will be established forever" (2 Samuel 7:12–16).

His coming would be accompanied by a special star or shining in the heavens. "I see him, but not now; I behold him, but not near. A star will come out of Jacob; a scepter will rise out of Israel" (Number 24:17).

He would be born in Bethlehem. "Bethlehem Ephrathah, though you are small among the clans of Judah, out of you will come for me one who will be ruler over Israel, whose origins are from of old, from ancient times" (Micah 5:2).

He would be born of a virgin. "The Lord himself will give you a sign: The virgin will be with child and will give birth to a son, and will call him Immanuel [God with us]" (Isaiah 7:14).

The Messiah would be a wonderful counselor, a mighty God, an everlasting Father, and a prince of peace; and he would reign on David's throne forever. "To us a child is born, to us a son is given,and the government will be on his shoulders.And he will be called Wonderful Counselor, Mighty God, Everlasting Father, Prince of Peace.Of the increase of his government and peace there will be no end. He will reign on David's throne and over his kingdom, establishing and upholding it with justice and righteousness from that time on and forever" (Isaiah 9:6–7).

He would come to Israel out of Egypt. "When Israel was a child, I loved him, and out of Egypt I called my son" (Hosea 11:1).

His birth would be accompanied by a great slaughter. "This is what the Lord says: 'A voice is heard in Ramah, mourning and great weeping, Rachel weeping for her children and refusing to be comforted, because her children are no more'" (Jeremiah 31:15).

A prophet would go before him in the wilderness, making a path for him to succeed. " A voice of one calling: 'In the desert prepare the way for the Lord; make straight in the wilderness a highway for our God'" (Isaiah 40:3).

He would set many people free, open the eyes of those in the dark, and preach good news. "The Spirit of the Sovereign Lord is on me, because the Lord has anointed me to preach good news to the poor. He has sent me to bind up the brokenhearted, to proclaim freedom for the captives and release from darkness for the prisoners, to proclaim the year of the Lord's favor and the day of vengeance of our God, to comfort all who mourn" (Isaiah 61:1–2).

He would be a healer and a Savior. "Strengthen the feeble hands, steady the knees that give way; say to those with fearful hearts, 'Be strong, do not fear; your God will come, he will come with vengeance; with divine retribution he will come to save you.' Then will the eyes of the blind be opened and the ears of the deaf unstopped. Then will the lame leap like a deer, and the mute tongue shout for joy" (Isaiah 35:3–6).

Galilee (the land of Zebulun and Naphtali) would see a great light. "There will be no more gloom for those who were in distress. In the past he humbled the land of Zebulun and the land of Naphtali, but in the future he will honor Galilee of the Gentiles, by the way of the sea, along the Jordan—the people walking in darkness have seen a great light; on those living in the land of the shadow of death a light has dawned" (Isaiah 9:1–2).

The Messiah would die at a specified time. The Old Testament prophet Daniel foretold the time of the coming and killing of the Messiah. It has been calculated to coincide with the time of Passover, 9 Nisan AD 30, the time Jesus died.

Truth 2

"Know and understand this: From the issuing of the decree to restore and rebuild Jerusalem [around 445 BC] until the Anointed One, the ruler, comes, there will be seven 'sevens,' and sixty-two 'sevens' [69 x 7 = 483 years]. It will be rebuilt with streets and a trench, but in times of trouble. After the sixty-two 'sevens,' the Anointed One will be cut off and will have nothing [approximately 9 Nisan AD 30, the death of Jesus]" (Daniel 9:25–26).

"Elijah" would come and prepare the way before the Messiah and turn the hearts of God's children back to their fathers. "I will send you the prophet Elijah before that great and dreadful day of the Lord comes. He will turn the hearts of the fathers to their children, and the hearts of the children to their fathers; or else I will come and strike the land with a curse" (Malachi 4:5–6).

Any Jew who studied prophecy in those days couldn't help but note the many levels on which God let people know when, where, and how the Messiah would be coming. God told the Jews:

- about Jesus's ancestors and his line of descent,

- that a special star (probably the Shekinah glory of God) would appear,

- what town the Messiah would be born in,

- that he would be born of a virgin,

- that he would be called Immanuel ("God with us"),

- who would pave the way for the Messiah,

- the places he would minister,

- that he would be a healer and a preacher of "good news," and

- the time of his demise.

What more could anyone ask from God to validate the coming of the Messiah—and that Jesus was that Messiah?

3

Jesus was TARGETED by Satan from the beginning.

Starting long before Jesus came into the world as Messiah, Satan tried to stop him from fulfilling his mission by ending Jesus's ancestral line. Consider this series of events:

In Genesis 3:15 God said, "I will put enmity between you and the woman, and between your offspring and hers; he will crush your head, and you will strike his heel."

This was God's first messianic promise. In it he assured Adam and Eve that despite their sin, one day a redeemer would come who would crush the head of Satan and destroy him forever. From that moment on Satan looked for this special "offspring." It seems he became obsessed with finding out who this would be and doing him in.

Genesis 4:1–16 tells the story of Cain and Abel. God warned Cain, "Sin is crouching at your door; it desires to have you, but you must master it" (Genesis 4:7). Later Cain killed his brother Abel. Perhaps this was the first attempt of Satan to terminate the line of Jesus, thinking righteous Abel would be the offspring through whom redemption would come. He wasn't, but Satan didn't know that.

As recorded in 1 Samuel 18:10–11, King Saul, tormented by an evil spirit, tried to kill David before he was even king: "An evil spirit from God came forcefully upon Saul. He was prophesying in his house, while David was playing the harp, as he usually did. Saul had a spear in his hand and he hurled it, saying to himself, 'I'll pin David to the wall.' But David eluded him twice."Saul was tormented by a demon for the rest of his life, and he repeatedly tried to kill David. It seems Satan knew David's line had been chosen for the Messiah and did his best at every turn to eliminate him. David faced many enemies throughout his life, including his own son Absalom, who led a rebellion against David and almost won. But God preserved David and his line and thwarted Satan's murderous plots.

In 1 Kings 12:1–24 we see how King Rehoboam, the son of Solomon, caused a split in the kingdom of Israel. Once again it seems Satan was working to end the messianic line. At one point Rehoboam barely escaped with his life when rebels threatened him.

Then, in 2 Kings 11:1 Satan again sought to destroy the Messiah by stamping out his family line. "When Athaliah the mother of Ahaziah saw that her son was dead, she proceeded to destroy the whole royal family." If Queen Athaliah had succeeded in killing off the royal line of David, the Messiah could not have come through it as prophesied. But the dead king's sister and her husband, the high priest, hid one little baby, Joash, who was heir to the throne. He survived, Athaliah was eventually killed, and the enemy was vanquished.

Later, as Jerusalem fell, it looked as if the king of Babylon would either kill all the remaining line of David or take them into captivity (see 2 Kings 25). Jehoiachin survived and the line went on, but Satan continued working to do all he could to eliminate it once and for all.

In those precarious years from the exile to Babylon to the time of the New Testament, the descendants of David lived in obscurity. But God ordained two members of the Davidic line, Joseph and Mary, to be the parents of the Messiah. Then, as soon as Jesus was born, Satan's attempts to kill the Messiah went into overdrive. King Herod ordered the slaughter of the innocents (see Matthew 2:16–18), and Jesus and his parents escaped by a hair—thanks to some divine intervention (see Matthew 2:13–15). Throughout Jesus's ministry Satan tried to halt the Savior's inexorable march to the cross.

The devil didn't succeed. Why? Because "the one who is in you is greater than the one who is in the world" (1 John 4:4).

4

Jesus's life was ACCURATELY recorded by eyewitnesses and inspired biographers.

Many Christians today believe several important principles about the Bible. First, that it's accurate in every way, whether you're talking science, history, conversations, details of actions, and so on.

Second, it's infallible. It never makes a mistake. You can trust it implicitly, explicitly, and all those other 'plicitlies.

Third, it was written by ordinary people, many of whom (such as Matthew, John, Peter, James, and Jude) were eyewitnesses to the facts and circumstances, and others (such as Luke and Paul) who did research and learned the facts and situations from eyewitnesses.

The question is, how did these ordinary people get everything right? Can it possibly be true that there are no mistakes anywhere, insofar as the original writings are concerned? Can we really trust the Bible completely to include truth on a higher level than that found by modern researchers?

Most Christians regard the Bible as the truth, the whole truth, and nothing but the truth, because ultimately it was authored by God. It records absolute truth that we can trust with our lives and our eternal souls.

For the deepest truths about Jesus and his ministry, we're depending on people like Matthew, Mark, Luke, and John, the writers of the four Gospels. How did they pull this off?

John explained in the gospel account that bears his name: "This is the disciple who testifies to these things and who wrote them down. We know that his testimony is true" (John 21:24). Later, in the book of 1 John, he wrote, "We are from God, and whoever knows God listens to us; but whoever is not from God does not listen to us. This is how we recognize the Spirit of truth and the spirit of falsehood" (1 John 4:6). If these words weren't true, they have an arrogance beyond what most writers would even dream of expressing. But John, the disciple who was too humble even to name himself in his own gospel, was deadly serious. "This is the truth," he said, "and if God is in you, and you know God, you'll know it as the truth" (my paraphrase).

Hmm.

Then there's Paul's statement to Timothy that "all Scripture is God-breathed and is useful for teaching, rebuking, correcting and training in righteousness" (2 Timothy 3:16). When Paul said "God-breathed," he meant that just as when you talk, you breathe over your vocal cords and sounds are produced, so the words of Scripture have the breath of God in them. And what happens when God breathes on something? It comes to life. That's why the author of the epistle to the Hebrews wrote, "The word of God is living and active" (Hebrews 4:12).

Those are powerful words, speaking of something—the Word of God—which is far more powerful than any engine, rocket, or explosive device in the world today. But the question is, how did they do it? How was it possible for these uneducated men to pen words containing the life of God so accurately that we can entrust our lives to their truths?

Jesus's own words in John 14:25–26 explain it: "All this I have spoken while still with you. But the Counselor, the Holy Spirit, whom the Father will send in my name, will teach you all things and will remind you of everything I have said to you."

There it is—the Holy Spirit would remind them. It's that simple. They could do their research, as Luke said he did (Luke 1:1–4). They could spin their theology. They could recite their stories. But when it came down to the nitty-gritty, there was only one person who could ensure they got it down right: the Spirit of God.

That's how the Bible came to us, and that's why we can trust it implicitly. Not just because good men wrote it. Not just because there were various eyewitnesses telling the same, cohesive story from different vantage points. But because the Spirit of God worked in their minds and hearts to be certain they remembered and restated it accurately.

What a book it is. It will change your life, if you let it.

5

Jesus's family tree INCLUDED murderers, sexual deviants, and genocidal maniacs.

It must have embarrassed Jesus on occasion. What, you ask? His forebears. Some of them were real hellions. Few were saints. A couple were genocidal maniacs.

How would you like those skeletons in your closet?

Probably all of us, at one time or another, have discovered an unsavory secret or two in our genealogical attics. I have only one that I know of, and my family rarely talks about it. When my dad casually asked the person involved about a certain relationship he had with another woman, Dad later told me, "He looked at me with such hatred in his eyes that I decided then and there never to bring it up again."

But really, this wasn't much. Perhaps my relative only engaged in a strange relationship. At worst, adultery. Compare that with the deeds done in some families, and it's almost laughable. Next to the fellow who has murder, lying, cheating, abuse, adultery, incest, and even genocide in his family tree, it's pretty mild.

But Jesus did have those things in his familial past. His genealogy in Matthew 1:1–16 gives us an astonishing insight into a Savior who had much to hide—if he had wanted to. But he didn't. He laid it all out for us—all the sinners, saints, and ain'ts of his family history.

There's Abraham, the ancient patriarch who lied twice to potentates to protect himself—and in so doing almost caused his wife to commit adultery against her will. His son Isaac did the same thing. And then there's Jacob, whose name essentially means "cheat"—which he did without flinching to nearly everyone dear to him.

Judah and his daughter-in-law Tamar committed incest. Ruth the Moabite, who was descended from the sexual union of Lot and his daughter, was a product of incest.

Next we find David, who committed adultery with Bathsheba and later had her husband murdered to cover it up. Solomon, the wisest, richest man who ever lived, in his last years deserted the God who made him wise and rich and became a pagan idolater. And Manasseh, later in the messianic lineage, gained the reputation of the bloodiest king in all Israel, murdering people left and right in his awful reign of terror. In fact, if you take a hard look at it, the sinners in Jesus's genealogy far outweigh the do-gooders by a wide margin.

Why is this? Why would the Savior of the world and King of heaven be burdened with such a tainted lineage? Perhaps for only one reason: Jesus was one of us. Perhaps God gave Jesus these forebears to remind us what he was sent to do: to save sinners.

Another beautiful truth is that many of those sinners in Jesus's family history also went down in history as some of God's greatest saints: Abraham, Isaac, Jacob, David . . . even Manasseh turned back to God at the end of his life.

Write it on a billboard if that's what it takes to really get it: all saints started out as sinners, and any sinner can become a saint—by simply entrusting himself or herself to the one in charge of the "Transformation Express."

6

Jesus truly was born
of a VIRGIN.

Nothing, it seems, has stirred more controversy than the Old Testament prophecy that Jesus would be born of a virgin. Scholars have argued about this for years; some, unable to believe God's power to accomplish such miracles, have pronounced that Mary must have made up the whole story after, perhaps, having an affair with a Roman soldier. What is the truth? Is there a clear way to discern God's intent and meaning regarding this prophecy?

This prophecy is recorded in Isaiah 7:14. It says, "The Lord himself will give you a sign: The virgin will be with child and will give birth to a son, and will call him Immanuel."

Isaiah spoke these words to King Ahaz, a descendant of David who sat on King David's throne in the nation of Judah. Ahaz was in trouble with Syria and Assyria. Security had been breached, and he and his nation were at risk of defeat and destruction. At God's behest, Isaiah told Ahaz that in sixty-five years the northern kingdom of Israel (Ephraim), which was also threatening him, would be broken. (This happened in 722 BC.)

God then challenged Ahaz to ask for any kind of sign in heaven or on earth to prove that this would happen. Ahaz refused to ask for a sign. So God chose a sign for him: a virgin would give birth to a child who would be called Immanuel, which means "God with us."

However, the Hebrew word for *virgin* is *almah,* which can also mean "young woman" or "maiden." We find the use of the word as "virgin" in such passages as Genesis 24:43; Proverbs 30:19; and Song of Solomon 1:3; 6:8. Nonetheless, the Hebrew word remained somewhat ambiguous— until the Septuagint came along.

The Septuagint was the Old Testament translated from Hebrew to Greek by seventy-two scholars in seventy-two days in Alexandria, Egypt, during the reign of Ptolemy Philadelphus (285–246 BC). The Septuagint was used by Jews in Egypt and throughout the Middle East because Greek, not Hebrew, was the language of the people. The word translators used for *almah* in the Septuagint is the Greek word *parthenos,* which unequivocally means "virgin." Other Greek words meant "young woman" or "maiden," but they were not used. Thus, through divine inspiration, those seventy-two scholars understood Isaiah's (and God's) intent that the meaning was more specific than just a young woman. God meant that the Messiah would be conceived by a virgin.

Matthew also quoted Isaiah from the Septuagint (Matthew 1:23). The word he used for *virgin* is also *parthenos.* This is the only time the passage is quoted in the New Testament, but Mary's exchange with the angel in Luke 1:34–37 makes it even clearer that this prophecy was about a virgin. That's how it was ultimately fulfilled—a virgin conceived a child through the power of the Most High. The baby born to that virgin, Mary, was the Son of God.

Though the Spirit of God may have allowed some ambiguity to King Ahaz about this virgin, he made it clear to the reader when the Septuagint was translated and when Matthew wrote under the Spirit's inspiration. People may argue about whether anyone can really be born of a virgin, or whether the story was made up. But the truth is that when it comes to an honest appraisal of the passages, the authors—and the Author—meant *virgin.*

Jesus's mother, Mary, felt the need to CONFIRM her call to bear God's Son.

Mary was a woman of faith. When the angel Gabriel came to her and told her she would soon be the mother of the Messiah, after just one question she submitted herself to the Lord. "'I am the Lord's servant,' Mary answered. 'May it be to me as you have said'" (Luke 1:38). Those are brave words for a young girl—many scholars believe she was only fourteen or fifteen years old at this time.

Yet at some point she wondered again how this could be true. It's always easier to worry in retrospect than at the time of the life-transforming event, isn't it?

Mary needed to talk to someone, to tell what had happened and get some advice, some confirmation that this was all true. But who?

Luke tells us: "Mary got ready and hurried to a town in the hill country of Judea, where she entered Zechariah's home and greeted Elizabeth" (Luke 1:39–40). When Gabriel had spoken to Mary about becoming the mother of the Son of God, he had told her about Elizabeth's miraculous pregnancy as well. He said, "Even Elizabeth your relative is going to have a child in her old age, and she who was said to be barren is in her sixth month. For nothing is impossible with God" (Luke 1:36–37).

Mary understood that this was another miracle. She must have known Elizabeth and visited her before at her home or seen her in

Jerusalem at the time of the Passover. Zechariah was a priest and would have served in the temple at times. In fact, he had been serving there when an angel appeared to him and told him he and Elizabeth would soon be parents, that they would have a baby who would be the Messiah's forerunner, John the Baptist. Perhaps Mary had even heard the news that Zechariah had been struck mute during his temple service—a consequence of his not immediately believing the angel's message.

Whatever Mary knew, she realized Elizabeth was the key to her own doubts. Elizabeth could assure her she wasn't imagining things, that the angel Gabriel had been real, and that what he had said would come to pass exactly as he had told her.

So she hurried to see this relative. Luke 1:41–45 tells of their meeting: "When Elizabeth heard Mary's greeting, the baby leaped in her womb, and Elizabeth was filled with the Holy Spirit. In a loud voice she exclaimed: 'Blessed are you among women, and blessed is the child you will bear! But why am I so favored, that the mother of my Lord should come to me? As soon as the sound of your greeting reached my ears, the baby in my womb leaped for job. Blessed is she who has believed that what the Lord has said to her will be accomplished!' "

In one fell swoop Elizabeth reconfirmed everything for Mary. She called Mary the "mother of my Lord," a clear acknowledgment of Mary's miraculous pregnancy and the holy identity of the baby she carried. Also, her own baby "leaped for joy" in her womb. That could only be another affirmation. And finally, she uttered a blessing on Mary and encouraged her to believe God's message to her.

Mary needed nothing more. She burst forth in a song of praise and ultimate faith and acceptance of her role in the eternal plan. It's known as "Mary's Song" or, in Latin, "The Magnificat." In this song Mary uttered profound words of faith, echoing Hannah in the Old Testament, whose pregnancy was also a miraculous gift from God (see 1 Samuel 1–2). Study the words of this song and you will see Mary as a woman of exuberant, potent faith, one who had all she needed to become the mother of the Messiah.

8

Other miraculous births support the TRUTH of Jesus's miraculous birth.

Mystery and controversy surround the topic of Jesus's virgin birth. In the natural it's impossible to believe. Human children are not born without a human mother and father. Even with today's scientific advances, genetic contributions by two human parents, male and female, are required for conception. The natural response would be to dismiss the Bible's account of Jesus's birth through a virgin as fiction, which many people do.

Some say Mary fabricated the whole story to cover up her illicit pregnancy. Of course, the problem with that is Joseph. When he found out Mary was pregnant, he knew the child was not his. He decided not to go through with the marriage (Matthew 1:18–20), but God changed his mind through a special dream in which he explained to Joseph that this baby was indeed God's Son, validating Mary's claims. The fact that Joseph married her and agreed with her story gives us two witnesses, not just one.

But skeptics persist. Some say the story of Jesus's virgin birth is a myth common in antiquity. The Greeks and Romans talked about gods mating with human women, but that's not the same as a virgin birth. The angel Gabriel told Mary, "The Holy Spirit will come upon you, and the power of the Most High will overshadow you. So the holy one to be born will be called the Son of God" (Luke 2:35). It doesn't talk about sex or a mating, just an "overshadowing," something not found in other ancient literature.

Even Mary, who came face to face with an angel, marveled at the announcement that she would give birth to God's Son: "'How will this be,' Mary asked the angel, 'since I am a virgin?'" (Luke 1:34).

Gabriel responded by explaining the basics of the awesome miracle of the Holy Spirit's work in Mary's life, but then he added something else which is significant as we wrestle with the hard-to-believe story of a virgin conception: he cited a readily verifiable account of another miraculous conception. Gabriel told Mary, "Even Elizabeth your relative is going to have a child in her old age, and she who was said to be barren is in her sixth month. For nothing is impossible with God" (Luke 1:36–37).

If Mary doubted the angel's story after he left her, she didn't have to doubt for long. She hurried to Elizabeth's house, where she discovered the angel's words were true. The elderly, long-childless woman was six months pregnant, and the baby, full of the Holy Spirit, further confirmed the miracle by leaping for joy within Elizabeth's womb. "Nothing is impossible with God," Gabriel had said. If God had caused this impossible pregnancy for Elizabeth, why could he not accomplish the miracle he had promised Mary—that she, a virgin, would give birth to the Son of God? Once we see and accept that God can work miracles, the difference between a miraculous birth and a virgin birth is just a matter of degrees.

Actually, miraculous conceptions and births seem to be one of God's specialties throughout the Bible. The first Hebrew, Abraham, was one hundred years old when his previously barren ninety-year-old wife conceived and gave birth to a son, Isaac, in precise fulfillment of God's promise. It's clear that both Abraham and Sarah understood this as a major miracle (see Genesis 18:10–15; 21:1–7). Their miraculously conceived son, Isaac, followed in the family tradition. Isaac's wife, Rebekah, was unable to conceive for twenty years until God answered Isaac's prayer. Rebekah conceived and gave birth to twins, Jacob and Esau (Genesis 25:19–26).

Jacob's wife Rachel was also childless. After the passage of time and many sons born to her rival, Leah, Genesis 30:22 tells us: "Then God remembered Rachel: he listened to her and opened her womb." Rachel conceived and gave birth to Joseph—who would one day preserve his family's lives during a famine—and later Benjamin (Genesis 30:22–24; 35:24). Although not virgin births, they were all miraculous gifts from God.

Then there was Samson. His mother had been sterile and childless until an angel visited with news that she would give birth to a special son who would be a Nazirite, separated and dedicated to God from his birth, and would begin to deliver Israel from its enemies (see Judges 13:2–5).

In 1 Samuel 1 we learn that Hannah's first son, Samuel, was also a miraculous gift from God. Second Kings 4:1–17 recounts the story of Elisha asking God to enable a barren woman and her elderly husband to conceive and, a year later, bear a son.

Some miraculous births came after desperately beseeching God to send a child in spite of impossible human situations. Other times people were surprised by the visit of angels with unexpected announcements of future births. We're given no background story on Samson's mother before the angel appeared to her. It seems Elizabeth and Zechariah had given up on ever being parents when the angel appeared to the old priest as he served God in the temple (Luke 1:5–25). Mary was an unmarried young teenager. Thoughts of a pregnancy would have been just as shocking as a visit by an angel.

What these episodes all have in common teaches us something that helps us better understand how God works. He often used miraculous births at pivotal points in history—when he was sending into the world a person who would introduce a new era or save his people. Abraham, Isaac, and Jacob were patriarchs—fathers of God's people. Joseph, sold into slavery in Egypt, rose to a position of power that allowed him to save his family and the Hebrew nation from a terrible famine. Samson started delivering God's people from the Philistines. Samuel was Israel's greatest judge, who presided over the birth of the Davidic dynasty from which came Jesus Christ.

Perhaps, to show beyond question that it was God who was saving and delivering his people, he chose to have these special people born in a special, supernatural, miraculous way. A child born to two young, healthy people is a child born in the ordinary way. But a child born to a woman who by then would have been a great-great-grandmother had she been able to conceive earlier—to a parent too old and a parent childless for decades—now that's a miracle. Everyone who heard about the miracles surrounding John the Baptist's birth "wondered about it, asking, 'What then is this child going to be?' For the Lord's hand was with him" (Luke 1:66).

Once we understand that God works miracles—sometimes in the conception of babies—accepting Christ's virgin birth is no stretch at all. I believe God still works miracles of conception today. I've known several couples who were unable to conceive until, through much prayer and help from doctors, they at last had a child. Mark it down and don't forget it: while there will never again be another virgin birth, God still blesses families with children, and especially those who have suffered through childlessness. It's a cause for thanksgiving, whether those children come through the womb or by adoption.

9

Jesus's parents were almost DIVORCED.

It's a classic story. Good teen in the neighborhood from a poor family is visited one night by an angel named Gabriel. Gabriel informs the girl, Mary, that she will be the mother of the Savior of the world (see Luke 1:26–38).

Mary, knowledgeable enough to understand how procreation happens, naturally wondered how this could be, since she was only engaged to a man but not yet married (or sexually intimate). The angel explained that the Holy Spirit would "overshadow" her, and the conception would occur miraculously.

It was kind of a good news/bad news situation for Mary. The good news was, the Savior of the world would come in her lifetime, and she'd be his mom. The bad news was, she'd probably be branded a loose woman; stories would circulate about her "insane angel story" and how her husband-to-be would divorce her before the wedding ceremony was ever performed.

Mary was definitely in a win-lose situation. Yet she asked only one question—how this might happen—and then bowed in submission to God. What faith she must have had!

Now think of her husband-to-be, Joseph. What would you do if the love of your life came to you with a tale like that? Probably exactly what Joseph decided to do: call off the wedding.

In those days being "betrothed" (engaged, in our terminology) was as legally binding as marriage: thus, dissolving such a contract was a divorce. Joseph was faced with two options according to Jewish law: have Mary stoned as an adulteress or give her a "certificate of dismissal," and end the betrothal quietly. Apparently Joseph believed in things like dignity, compassion, and love rather than in vengeance, and he chose to divorce Mary without fanfare—a course few of his generation would have taken.

It must have been a terrible moment. This young couple—perhaps neither was older than sixteen or seventeen—saw the ending of their lives before they'd even begun. And to top it off, it seemed Joseph would have to deal with an ex who couldn't accept the truth but rather persisted in telling some whopper about the Holy Spirit. Did people call her "Crazy Mary," or something equally insulting?

Nevertheless, God, being himself compassionate, gracious, and faithful, did not hang Joseph and Mary out to dry. No, he sent an angel in a dream to convince Joseph of the truth (see Matthew 1:18–25). The angel shared the same divine plan with Joseph and even told him what to name the baby: Jesus. After Joseph awoke, he took Mary as his wife. As far as we know, he said no more about it; but you can probably imagine his relief. "Sorry, I didn't believe you the first time around, Mary, but you have to admit, it's a humdinger of a story!"

Throughout history, skeptics have derided the account of the virgin birth as a myth foisted on us by gullible people. But the truth is, even Mary and Joseph were skeptical at first. They didn't just blindly buy into this Holy Spirit–conception idea. Both had questions, and both faced the reality of what they were being asked to do. Quite likely, the question of exactly how Mary got pregnant out of wedlock hung over many a conversation with friends and at every family gathering throughout the couple's married lives. It wouldn't be put to rest for many years, until Jesus himself had risen from the dead and proven himself to be the Savior of the world. Even in light of this, some refuse to believe.

In each of our lives, God will ask us to do something that, while probably less difficult or unusual than what he asked of Mary and Joseph, may feel every bit as tough and absurd in the context of our own lives. And it will require a measure of faith. Will we be up to it?

God never flinches from our honest questions. Nor does he condemn us for our skepticism. He made sure Mary and Joseph had the assurance they needed. Their response—obedient trust and faith—won God's wholehearted support, and they went on to be the revered couple that brought Jesus into the world.

Jesus could lay claim to both humanity and deity through his miraculous birth. But that means he did have to struggle with real life as a human. Did Jesus have to live with gossip and put-downs about his mother? I think he probably did. And yet he persevered in his mission to save the world—despite the rumors, gossip, and hatred. He overcame all because his human faith in his heavenly Father kept him strong in the battle from the beginning to the end.

10

A Roman emperor played an IMPORTANT role in Jesus's birth.

Imagine the unpleasantness of being forced by the government to make a journey of three or more days to register in a census. Now imagine making the journey along sandy, rough dirt roads on foot or on the back of a donkey—while pregnant. Makes you appreciate your government, your SUV, and Holiday Inn a little more, doesn't it? Both Mary and Joseph were descendants of David, whose hometown was Bethlehem. That meant a long trip from Nazareth necessitated by the decree of Rome's emperor, Caesar Augustus.

Luke 2:1–5 explains it this way: "In those days Caesar Augustus issued a decree that a census should be taken of the entire Roman world. (This was the first census that took place while Quirinius was governor of Syria.) And everyone went to his own town to register. So Joseph also went up from the town of Nazareth in Galilee to Judea, to Bethlehem the town of David, because he belonged to the house and line of David. He went there to register with Mary, who was pledged to be married to him and was expecting a child."

The place of the Messiah's birth was dictated by a royal whim—an edict from the most powerful ruler on earth. Or was it?

Centuries earlier the most powerful ruler in heaven and earth had made another decree concerning the birth of the Messiah: "Bethlehem

Ephrathah, though you are small among the clans of Judah, out of you will come for me one who will be ruler over Israel, whose origins are from of old, from ancient times" (Micah 5:2).

Proverbs 21:1 helps explains how Caesar's edict echoed God's and helped bring it to fruition: "The king's heart is in the hand of the Lord; he directs it like a watercourse wherever he pleases."

All the ways of mankind are in the hands of God. He chooses who lives and who dies, who becomes rich and who ends up poor, who lives to be eighty and who dies as a teenager. God is working in the world at all times and in all lives to accomplish his will. As Psalm 33:9–11 says, "He spoke, and it came to be; he commanded, and it stood firm. The Lord foils the plans of the nations; he thwarts the purposes of the peoples. But the plans of the Lord stand firm forever, the purposes of his heart through all generations."

Or as Isaiah 45:5–7 says, "I am the Lord, and there is no other; apart from me there is no God. I will strengthen you, though you have not acknowledged me, so that from the rising of the sun to the place of its setting men may know there is none besides me. I am the Lord, and there is no other. I form the light and create darkness, I bring prosperity and create disaster; I, the Lord, do all these things."

Clearly, Caesar was no grand potentate to God the Father. His control over the life of Jesus and his parents was merely an illusion. He was merely a useful cog in the machinery that God used to bring the Messiah into the world in the way he had foreknown and foreordained.

11

Jesus may NOT have been born in a stable.

Another interesting truth you might notice in reading the story of Jesus's birth is that there's never any mention of a stable: "The time came for the baby to be born, and she gave birth to her firstborn, a son. She wrapped him in cloths and placed him in a manger, because there was no room for them in the inn" (Luke 2:6–7).

Later the angels told shepherds in the hills of a sign by which they'd recognize the newborn king: "You will find a baby wrapped in cloths and lying in a manger" (Luke 2:12).

Mary "wrapped him in cloths," a tradition at that time (and still done in many places in the Middle East) believed to keep the baby from injuring himself through scratching or poking with his own fingernails. Some also believed it strengthened the child's limbs. Parents who didn't do this were considered negligent (see Ezekiel 16:4).

Then Mary "placed him in a manger, because there was no room for them in the inn." From the idea of Jesus's being placed in a cow's or sheep's feed trough (manger), it has been surmised through the ages that Mary gave birth to Jesus in a stable. But we don't know that for sure.

Today in Bethlehem you can visit the Church of the Nativity in a grotto. The church is really a cave, and it's possible the place Christ was born was also a stone-hewn cave. But again, nothing tells us for sure one way or another.

However and wherever Jesus was born, he entered this world in a humble and lowly fashion. This wasn't the Mayo Clinic or a birthing room fit for a great king. Jesus may have started at the bottom of the heap so none of us could claim he had it easier than we do.

12

Jesus's birth probably was not announced by SINGING angels.

From "Hark! The Herald Angels Sing" to "Joy to the World" and "Silent Night," Christmas songs help spread images of angelic hosts singing gloriously at the birth of Jesus. *Messiah,* Handel's masterwork, even pictured them singing choruses from heaven.

One problem: the Bible never says they sang.

Take a look at the passage. Luke 2:8–14 says, "There were shepherds living out in the fields nearby, keeping watch over their flocks at night. An angel of the Lord appeared to them, and the glory of the Lord shone around them, and they were terrified. But the angel said to them, 'Do not be afraid. I bring you good news of great joy that will be for all the people. Today in the town of David a Savior has been born to you; he is Christ the Lord. This will be a sign to you: You will find a baby wrapped in cloths and lying in a manger.' Suddenly a great company of the heavenly host appeared with the angel, praising God and saying, 'Glory to God in the highest, and on earth peace to men on whom his favor rests.'"

Notice that the two times an angel or angels speak, the biblical author used the words *said* and *saying.* It seems the angels did not sing; they spoke.

It's not that angels can't sing. The first time angels are recorded as singing is during Creation, when God finished making the heavens and the earth:"Where were you when I laid the earth's foundation? Tell me, if you understand. Who marked off its dimensions? Surely you know! Who stretched a measuring line across it? On what were its footings set, or who laid its cornerstone—while the morning stars sang together and all the angels shouted for joy?" (Job 38:4–7).

"Morning stars" is a term often used of angels.

The next time we find a reference to angels singing is in Revelation 5:8–10, where we're given the text of a song that will be sung by four living creatures (angels) and twenty-four elders (humans): "They sang a new song: 'You are worthy to take the scroll and to open its seals, because you were slain, and with your blood you purchased men for God from every tribe and language and people and nation. You have made them to be a kingdom and priests to serve our God, and they will reign on the earth.'"

Why the apparent long hiatus between songs? Perhaps the angels sang before sin entered the world and only again after sin was paid for by Christ. Perhaps they didn't sing while the plan of redemption was unfolding because joy, their cause for breaking forth into song, comes only when people are redeemed and saved.

13

Jesus's birth held SPECIAL significance for the shepherds.

The first people beyond Joseph and Mary to receive the announcement of Jesus's birth were the shepherds, watching their flocks in the hills above Bethlehem.

Wait a second. Did you get that? Shepherds?

Gabriel the angel came to Mary and possibly to Joseph personally. But shouldn't he or some other important angel have gone next to the leaders of the Jews? To the high priest? To the king? Or at least to the ancient *Jerusalem Post* reporters: "Hey, better get down to Bethlehem, guys. Seems something big is happening there!"

But no. God didn't send his angels to such important personages, who could have gotten the word out literally all over the known world. Instead, he sent them to some lonely shepherds, probably swapping stories and playing their pipes around a campfire, maybe a little bored or grimacing at the smell of the sheep when the wind shifted. These men and boys, and perhaps a few daughters, hurried down after the angels' appearance to see the baby in the manger. But they probably did little to let others know what they saw; perhaps Luke only found out about their special revelation when he began interviewing witnesses for his gospel. We don't really know what they did with the angelic news, but it's probably fair to say they didn't run over to Herod's throne and give him the news of the coming of the Messiah.

The question is, why make a special announcement to these shepherds? Why not someone important or with some real power to help or at least protect the baby?

The shepherds more than likely guarded the sheep used in the daily sacrifices at the temple in Jerusalem. They must have understood their mission well: these had to be the most perfect, best-kept sheep in all of Israel, because they would be the atoning gifts worshipers brought to make a payment for their sins in God's house. None of these sheep could be harmed, hurt, broken, or lost.

These shepherds took their work seriously. The Bible says they were "watching" over their flocks. They weren't off playing games, hitting the local casinos, or drinking at the pub. They stood there, on duty, ready to ward off any attack.

Yet these were ordinary people: "the last" of Jesus's famous phrase, "The first shall be last, and the last first." And I think that's one important reason God sent angels to these people in particular: because they weren't much different than we.

Repeatedly the Bible tells us Jesus didn't come for the self-righteous. He said it was harder for rich people to get into his kingdom than a "camel through the eye of a needle." And he made clear that he came specifically for "those who were sick"—or, more simply, for plain old brown-wrapper sinners.

For you and me. Maybe if we had been there that night, the angels might have spoken to us too.

14

Jesus's birth date was not
DECEMBER 25, AD 0.

Was December 25, AD 0 the birthdate of Jesus?

When you study the records, these are the things you quickly discover: Jesus was born when Herod the Great was still alive, because we know Herod tried to kill him (see Matthew 2:1–18). Herod the Great reigned from about 37 to 4 BC. That would put Jesus's birth no later than 4 BC. And since the Bible mentions nothing about Herod's health at the time—from the record, he appears to be in pretty good shape—it might have been as much as two years earlier, because Herod died after a long illness. That would put Jesus's birth around 5 to 6 BC.

According to Luke 2:1 Caesar Augustus ordered that a census should be taken of the Roman Empire. Consulting various records, we know of two censuses taken during that period, one in 8 BC and one in AD 6, as the census was taken every fourteen years (primarily to locate young men to fill the Roman legions). Although Jews were normally exempt from the census because they couldn't become soldiers, it's still likely they would have registered at those times. Nonetheless, the AD 6 date is too late because Herod was dead by then. And 8 BC seems rather early for Jesus's birth. Many scholars suggest that it might have taken several years to get all the records in order, and that leaves us near 6 BC again.

Quirinius was governor of Syria at the same time, according to Luke

2:2. But we know that Quirinius governed Syria from AD 6–9, again too late. However, a stone fragment found near Rome in AD 1764 speaks of a governor who served two different times over Syria. Based on the description, this could only have been Quirinius. Again, this points back to a birth after 6 BC and before the end of 4 BC.

We know no other details of Jesus's birth—whether it was in the winter (as in December) or what the actual date was. December 25 came to be celebrated as Jesus's birth date sometime before AD 336, when someone unearthed a Roman almanac report listing that date. Saturnalia, a Roman holiday in midwinter (December 17), was celebrated with merriment and gift-giving. December 25 was also the birth date of the Iranian mystery god Mithra, known as the Sun of Righteousness. All these dates—and the need in Christendom for a Christian celebration—eventually led to fixing the celebration of Christ's birth on December 25, but it has nothing to do with the actual history of his birth. (As a side note on this, the Orthodox churches of the East celebrate Christ's birth on January 7, a tradition that also has a long history behind it.)

Despite the fact that we have little evidence to back up December 25 as Jesus's birth date, he was born on some day. It might seem we should celebrate on a date that has some real facts behind it, but we don't really have any information about the date. We don't even know whether it was winter in Israel when Joseph and Mary traveled.

The early Christians apparently didn't think it was an important event, although we do read that famous people's birthdays were times of celebration. Still, though the Christmas tradition has no real biblical roots, it remains wise to remember Jesus's birth as well as his death. We may have gone a little overboard in our spending for this holiday, but look at it this way: gift-giving is the one biblically established event surrounding the birth of Jesus—he received presents from the wise men. And certainly the giving of gifts to each other in remembrance of God's greatest Gift of all is a happy way of giving back to him as the ultimate object of our worship and love.

15

PERSIAN kingmakers declared Jesus king.

When the Magi, or "wise men," arrived in Jerusalem, they created quite a stir. Matthew says that King Herod was "disturbed," and the whole city with him. In fact, anytime Herod became disturbed, everyone knew blood would flow. He had committed many murders protecting his throne, and he would order many more. The city reacted in fear of Herod. But Herod was disturbed about the Magi.

Who were these people, and how did they provoke such a furor?

Scholars believe they might have been a party of three (although they probably had an army escort, with numerous slaves and assistants) because they gave Jesus three gifts: gold, frankincense, and myrrh. But we don't know for sure. What we do know is that they probably were from Persia—astrologers, possibly from the Zoroastrian religion of the East. These astrologers go back as far as the time of Daniel, and that's really where the interesting part of this story begins.

Daniel, a Jewish captive taken to Babylon to serve in the king's court, was placed in charge of the wise men there after he interpreted a dream for King Nebuchadnezzar (see Daniel 2:48; 5:11). These were the Magi, who served in the court of the king.

Although the book of Daniel does not specifically say so, since Daniel was the leader of this group, it's likely he told them many of the prophecies and truths from the Old Testament. Perhaps one of the things he shared with them was the fact that the Messiah of Israel would be heralded by a special star in the heavens (see Numbers 24:17), since these men had a strong interest in the stars. Perhaps over time some of these people became believers in the God of Daniel; it's even possible that a sect arose that awaited the appearance of the star.

It's not too difficult to imagine that these wise men visiting Jerusalem were descendants of those from Daniel's day who continued to look for this star. When they saw it in the heavens, they somehow knew it was the same star they'd been looking for. Though some have supposed this star was a comet or supernova, more than likely, since it moved, it was a manifestation of the Shekinah, or glory of God. This would have been the same kind of light that guided Israel as they traveled from Egypt to Canaan (see Exodus 13:21).

Thus, when the Magi arrived in Jerusalem looking for the one who had been born king of the Jews, Herod was worried. But why? Why would some astrologers scare him?

First, they were powerful men: they may even have been kings themselves (see Psalm 72:10; Isaiah 49:7; 60:3). Imagine the impact these men and their entourage would have had on the heart of Herod's realm. But it seems the most important reason Herod feared the Magi was due to the important role they played in selecting kings and powerful rulers. It was the Magi who named the kings in Babylon. They were kingmakers with power to exalt and power to humble. Their acceptance and blessing on a new king was all that was needed to guarantee his ascendancy. The mere fact that three notable Magi from the East came to find out about Israel's new king and worship him told the story: he was greater than they were, and worthy of their utmost respect and fealty.

No wonder Herod was disturbed. These Magi recognized Jesus as the king of the Jews. They came to pronounce their blessing on the new king and worship him.

16

Jesus received THREE gifts from the wise men.

The "wise men" (or Magi) brought three gifts to Jesus: gold, frankincense, and myrrh (see Matthew 2:11). This is the main reason scholars believe there were three of them, but it's possible there were more or fewer (but there were at least two, since Matthew 2:1 refers to them in the plural). But why these three gifts? And what was the real value of these treasures?

Gold retains its value even today. At around three hundred dollars per ounce now, a bag or box of gold would have bought many resources and necessities in those days. Also, the wise men recognized Jesus to be a king—king of the Jews (see Matthew 2:2)—and gold was a gift worthy of a great ruler.

Frankincense is also valuable. Much of the wealth that came out of Arabia and India was related to this resin, taken from the bark of the terebinth tree. Israelite priests used the bitter-tasting but aromatic spice in the creation of the holy oil used in temple ceremonies (see Exodus 30:34–36). Priests also burned it in the grain-offering sacrifices of Hebrew worship (see Leviticus 6:15). Frankincense symbolized spiritual fervor, according to Malachi 1:11. It was an appropriate gift that foreshadowed Christ's role as high priest of Israel and the mediator of our salvation.

The third gift, myrrh, was the resin of a shrublike tree that grows in the Arabian deserts and Africa. Gum drips onto the ground and forms an oily, yellowish substance that can be collected and used for cosmetics, holy oil, and other aromatic materials. The soldiers gave Jesus myrrh to stanch his pain as he died on the cross, but Christ refused it (see Mark 15:23). Nicodemus and Joseph of Arimathea also used it to prepare Jesus's body for burial. It was used to cover the odor of decay in the hot Middle Eastern climate. The wise men presented myrrh to Jesus, foreshadowing his death on the cross.

The three gifts are highly symbolic. Gold for a king; frankincense for a priest; myrrh for a sacrificing Savior. Did the wise men know this was Jesus's destiny? We can't be sure. Clearly, they understood much about the Christ child that their contemporaries completely missed.

What happened to the three gifts? We know Jesus had no wealth or fortune when he began his ministry, so the gifts had long since disappeared or been used up. Since Joseph and Mary fled to Egypt shortly after Jesus's birth and remained there for a while, they may have used the gifts to finance their daily living: perhaps Joseph was unable to work there. When they returned to Israel, they may have used what remained to set Joseph up in his carpentry business or to buy a home. We just don't know.

But it is in the spirit of those gifts that we give presents to loved ones as we celebrate Christmas.

17

Insecure LEADERS wanted to kill Jesus—even as a baby.

Jesus's birth is strange enough. Lying in a manger, wrapped in rags . . . you know the story. It makes a great narrative, but few would willingly choose such a humble, uncomfortable beginning.

But the real drag was how Jesus had barely gotten started in life before insecure leaders were already worried he threatened their power—and tried to kill him! What made a powerful king like Herod the Great fear a baby? The answer is found in Matthew 2:1–18. Herod the Great, the first of the Herodians who ruled Israel from 37–4 BC, never seemed all that secure in his power, in spite of his successes. He lived an exciting life of opulence and plenty. He undertook vast building projects, trying to create lasting monuments to his name and greatness. Many of the ruins you can visit in Jerusalem today come from the time and the imagination of Herod the Great. But he was a suspicious and paranoid ruler, partly because, as a descendant of Esau and not a full-fledged Jew, the Jews never accepted him. He was so insecure, seeing rivals to his throne and plots against him even when there were none, that no one was safe—not even his own family. He executed at least three of his sons and one of his wives.

But Herod's greatest claim to infamy was his pursuit of the Messiah. This resulted from a murderous desire to make sure no one succeeded him as king except those he designated. When Jesus was born in Bethlehem and wise men from the East came to Jerusalem searching for him, Herod gave them a personal audience. He learned about the star they'd seen, indicating the arrival of the Messiah, and he also learned from the lawyers and scribes where this child was to be born: in Bethlehem. Matthew says that Herod secretly called these wise men to a consultation, told them the child would be found in Bethlehem, and asked them to report back to him once they'd found the baby. He lied, telling them that he wanted to know so that he could go and worship the child also.

Why Herod trusted the wise men and didn't send his officers right away we don't know. Perhaps he thought the wise men would do the dirty work of finding the kid, which could be a rather arduous procedure, and then when they came back to him, he could get rid of the boy rather easily.

So the wise men went to Bethlehem, found Jesus and his parents (now probably living in a house or in the home of a relative), and worshiped the boy as the promised Messiah. But they were warned in a dream not to go back to Herod, so they returned home by another route, avoiding Herod altogether. When Herod heard that the wise men had disobeyed him, he became furious: "He gave orders to kill all the boys in Bethlehem and its vicinity who were two years old and under, in accordance with the time he had learned from the Magi" (Matthew 2:16).

Bethlehem was a small village just outside Jerusalem. While its fame rested on the fact that King David had been born and lived there, at the time of Jesus's birth it was little more than a bump in the road. However, because of its proximity to Jerusalem, this slaughter of Herod's could have involved hundreds of children from Bethlehem too. Matthew quoted a prophecy from the prophet Jeremiah, saying Herod's actions had fulfilled it: "A voice is heard in Ramah, weeping and great mourning, Rachel weeping for her children and refusing to be comforted, because they are no more" (Matthew 2:18; see also Jeremiah 31:15).

Joseph and Mary managed to escape this carnage with Jesus because, before it started, God warned them in a dream to flee to Egypt. But questions comes to mind: Why did God let this crazy king kill all those little children? Why didn't he have Herod die before the wise men finished their journey or find some other way to thwart the murderous plot?

Perhaps it's because Herod wasn't the ultimate culprit in this case. Behind Herod stood Herod's primary instigator, Satan. And Satan would not have been stopped with some easy remedy like the death of Herod. His desire to murder Jesus would continue from this moment until Jesus's actual death on the cross.

Still, even Satan couldn't thwart God's plan. Jesus died, yes, and for the sins of the whole world, acquiring for us the greatest gift anyone can ever receive: redemption. Then he rose again, showing he had conquered death permanently. You may wonder at the opposition you face as a Christian trying to help others and reach out in ministry. But don't worry about the attacks. Rebuff them when it's appropriate. Otherwise, just plod on, doing the work, knowing God will ensure his plan succeeds.

18

Jesus is the REASON for Xmas (and other historic symbols).

Probably every person has seen the shortened version of *Christmas:* Xmas. Why do we do this? Is it an attempt to "take Christ out of Christmas," as some charge?

The Greek spelling of Christ is *Xristos*. The first letter is a chi, which has a *ch* sound. Xristos means "Christ" or "Messiah" or "Anointed One." Xmas is just a shortened way of saying, Xristos-mas, or Christmas.

Perhaps you've also seen the symbol of the fish. Some Christians put this symbol on their cars or doors. In the early days of Christianity, believers were persecuted by the Roman Empire. To help Christians locate other believers who would help them, they developed a secret code or sign language. The fish was one symbol that identified Christians to other Christians. The Greek word for *fish* is *ichthus* (pronounced, ik-thoos). This word was an anagram for a number of Greek terms:

   I = Iesus = Jesus
 CH = Xristos = Christ
 TH = Theos = God (as in "theology" or "theocratic")
  U = Uios (pronounced *we-ose*) = Son
  S = Soter (pronounced *So-tare*) = Savior

Thus, the ichthus was a symbol indicating "Jesus Christ, Son of God,

Savior." It was a sure way to find people who would help you when you were hiding from Roman persecutors.

Another well-known symbol is the cross. People wear cross pendants, cross earrings, cross rings, and so on. The cross was an instrument of death. It would be like someone today wearing a symbol of an electric chair on a necklace, or a needle replicating that used in lethal injection. However, because of Jesus's sacrifice and resurrection, the empty cross came to symbolize salvation and faith in Jesus. Catholic crosses also feature the figure of Jesus. But the empty cross, the Protestant version, represents the fact that Jesus didn't stay on the cross but arose—defeating death—and is alive today in heaven.

Other symbols of Christ's birth and life are still common today: angels with wings spread to symbolize the angels who announced Jesus's birth; a shepherd's crook to represent Jesus as the Good Shepherd; the descending dove pictures the Holy Spirit; and a candle's flame reminds us of the Holy Spirit's coming with fire on the day of Pentecost.

While we must guard against letting such important symbols become trivialized, they can be good ways to communicate what we believe. Just wearing one of these symbols can often open lines of fellowship with other believers or opportunities to share our faith with those we meet.

19

Jesus came from the WRONG side of the tracks.

One of the prophecies about Jesus that often is overlooked is found in Matthew 2:23: "He will be called a Nazarene." Although Mary and Joseph took Jesus and fled to Egypt to escape King Herod's mad campaign to kill him—along with all the male children in Bethlehem—they returned to Israel after Herod's death, settling in Nazareth to avoid Herod's troublesome son, Archelaus.

Today a whole denomination of the Christian church is known as the Church of the Nazarene. Their unique doctrine centers on holiness, godliness, and remaining separate from the world. But that's a far cry from what it meant to be a Nazarene in Jesus's day.

Nazareth had a reputation as a place of riffraff because it functioned as a stop on some major trade routes through the Middle East. Merchants, prostitutes, Roman soldiers, and others gathered there for drinking, festivity, and all kinds of sin. Nazarenes were generally despised, even to the point that the very word became an insult.

The prophecy that Jesus would be called a Nazarene is not found in the Old Testament, though some believe it might have referred to the word *branch* in Isaiah 11:1. But there must have been a common tradition about the Messiah, because when Nathaniel heard about Jesus from Philip, the first thing he said was, "Nazareth! Can anything good come from there?" (John 1:46). The Jews passed down many things verbally (many of which can be found in the Jewish Talmud, the rabbis' commentary on the books of the Law) that never made it into the canon of Scripture.

The idea that the Messiah would be regarded as riffraff and worse comes from several prophecies in the Old Testament:

- "I am a worm and not a man, scorned by men and despised by the people. All who see me mock me; they hurl insults, shaking their heads: 'He trusts in the LORD; let the LORD rescue him. Let him deliver him, since he delights in him.'"(Psalm 22:6–8)

- "This is what the LORD says—the Redeemer and Holy One of Israel—to him who was despised and abhorred by the nation." (Isaiah 49:7)

- "He was despised and rejected by men, a man of sorrows, and familiar with suffering. Like one from whom men hide their faces he was despised, and we esteemed him not." (Isaiah 53:3)

From these passages it's clear that Jesus would be despised and hated, which he was—and still is by many people today. So when someone learned he was from Nazareth, it all made sense.

But I wonder why Jesus put up with insults and rejection? I think the reason is clear: Jesus was one of us. If we face rejection and censure because of our race, looks, heritage, or nationality, we can know that Jesus also knew what it was to deal with such difficulties. He didn't let people's insults affect him but responded with integrity and love, always reaching out—even to those who criticized him the most—hoping that some spark might be fanned into flame in their hearts by the reality of his love, not the shape of his nose.

20

Jesus had REAL brothers and sisters.

Was Jesus an only child? Though some today believe that Mary, the mother of Jesus, remained a virgin all her life, the New Testament seems to indicate otherwise. A number of references are made to Jesus and his brothers. For instance, Mark 3:32–35 says, "A crowd was sitting around him [Jesus], and they told him, 'Your mother and brothers are outside looking for you.' 'Who are my mother and my brothers?' he asked. Then he looked at those seated in a circle around him and said, 'Here are my mother and my brothers. Whoever does God's will is my brother and sister and mother.'" This event is also recorded in Matthew 12:46–50 and Luke 8:19–21.

But another passage goes even further. In Matthew 13:55–56 we're told the people of Jesus's hometown commented on his miracles, saying, "Isn't this the carpenter's son? Isn't his mother's name Mary, and aren't his brothers James, Joseph, Simon and Judas? Aren't all his sisters with us?"

So here we have clear evidence that Jesus had at least four brothers and more than one sister. Were these the children of Mary or, as some have suggested, children of Joseph's from a previous marriage?

It seems to make sense that if these brothers and sisters were someone other than Mary's children, the text would say so. Furthermore, if Mary remained a virgin all her life, that, too, seems to be a point the New

Testament would make. Instead, we have Matthew 1:24–25, which says, "When Joseph woke up, he did what the angel of the Lord had commanded him, and took Mary home as his wife. But he had no union with her until she gave birth to a son. And he gave him the name Jesus." This indicates that Mary remained a virgin only until Jesus's birth. Thereafter she engaged in a normal marriage to her husband, producing other natural children.

21

Jesus's parents DIDN'T understand him.

Luke 2:41–51 tells a story—the only time it's recorded in Scripture—of Jesus and his family visiting Jerusalem for the Passover celebration. This was a long trip for them, and the roads in those days were fraught with danger. Usually, as happened in this case, people traveled together in a caravan. This meant protection from robbers and a safe journey for all.

Luke says nothing about what the family did together when they reached their destination; he skips ahead and tells us that after the feast, everyone left. Except Jesus. He stayed behind, apparently without telling his parents. (He may have told them and, like any distracted parent with several small children, perhaps they just weren't really listening. But we don't know that. I just know that's what would probably happen with my kid.)

After traveling for a whole day, Mary and Joseph started looking around for their eldest son. Surely he was somewhere among their family in the caravan. After all, he was probably a friendly guy, and at twelve years old he would be quite normal in wanting to distance himself from the old fogies in the crowd (in a sinless way, of course). When they didn't locate him immediately, the antennae went up—suddenly everyone began looking for Jesus. They couldn't find him, and Joseph and Mary, probably entrusting the rest of their children to aunts and uncles, retraced their path back to Jerusalem looking for Jesus. Surely they must have feared he'd been harmed.

They didn't find him on the road back to the city, which took them a whole day to travel. They spent the next two days combing through Jerusalem, calling out for their son, asking questions, describing the boy to strangers, and getting shrugs and shakes of the head all the way. Where was he? What had happened?

Finally they came to the temple itself, and there they found him— sitting in the middle of a crowd of rabbis, not only asking questions but also stunning everyone with his learned and artful answers. Everyone was amazed at all this child knew about God, the Torah, and the prophets. They couldn't believe he was only twelve years old.

I picture Mary and Joseph just standing there with their mouths open, first astonished that their son could blow away this group of scholars, and second appalled at how much time they'd lost, forcing them to travel alone back to their home country. Joseph, a typical father, gaped and rubbed his beard. But Mary, like most mothers, had something to say. "Son, why have you treated us like this? Your father and I have been anxiously searching for you" (Luke 2:48).

So Jesus's parents' first question wasn't about what he'd done that was noteworthy or remarkable but about how they'd been treated? Be that as it may, Mary had a point. Shouldn't a twelve-year-old, no matter how mature, keep the folks informed of his whereabouts and what he plans to do? My wife grills my sixteen-year-old daughter about every step she takes outside our house—who she'll be with, who's driving, whether someone's parents will be present . . . it goes on and on. So it's not as though Mary was out of line with this particular line of questioning.

But how does Jesus reply? Luke 2:49 tells us: "Why were you searching for me?" he asked. "Didn't you know I had to be in my Father's house?"

It may sound a little impudent on the face of it, maybe even arrogant. But remember: Jesus, for twelve years, had lived an exemplary life. No tantrums. No rebellions. No badmouthing Mom or Dad. No wrong ever done, ever. He was the model kid. I'm sure Mary and Joseph both bragged plenty about how little trouble Jesus was and what a handful the others were in comparison. And then this—an almost defiant act of disobedience.

Or was it?

We could say Jesus simply forgot himself. It was such fun talking and teaching that it slipped his mind that everyone else had headed for home. It was an honest mistake.

But still seemingly a mistake. And yet perhaps not a sin. Sin involves willful disobedience. That would mean Jesus had meant to disobey their command. But what if there was no command? Maybe his parents just assumed he would join the caravan with the rest of them. So perhaps it was a mistake on their part.

And who knows? Maybe Jesus had been talking about this trip for weeks, making noise about how much he wanted to go to the temple and be "in his Father's house." Maybe if they had been listening, they would have been more aware of his needs and concerns. This wasn't just about them, after all.

The point is, while at first it may seem like rank disobedience, it was anything but that. The text says that neither Mary nor Joseph understood what Jesus meant by his reply. It also tells us that Jesus went on from there "and was obedient to them," meaning when they did give the command, he obeyed to the letter and spirit of their law. And last, Luke tells us that Mary "treasured these things in her heart."

Remember that Mary and Joseph were dealing with a one-of-a-kind, totally unique, never-before-seen kind of human being. Because of the revelations surrounding Jesus's birth, perhaps they should have known, as Jesus implied, where he would be and that he would be doing some unique things with his time and schedule.

So while we can't pin a sin to Jesus's record, we can say that maybe communication between him and his parents wasn't always perfect. And that's something all of us can identify with.

22

Jesus "LEARNED" obedience.

Did Jesus learn anything in his human incarnation? Since, as God, he was omniscient, what could he possibly learn from our world?

As a human being Jesus grew four ways (according to Luke 2:52): "in wisdom and stature, and in favor with God and men." If you look at those four categories, you can see the four basic ways any person has to mature and develop:

1. in wisdom—mentally
2. in stature—physically
3. in favor with God—spiritually
4. in favor with men—socially

This sums up Jesus's maturing process rather nicely. But what could he have learned?

Hebrews 5:8–9 helps illuminate what Jesus might have come to understand and apply in his life: "Although he was a son, he learned obedience from what he suffered and, once made perfect, he became the source of eternal salvation for all who obey him."

Obedience? That's what Jesus learned?

Yes, and what an important lesson. From 1 Corinthians 11:3 we

55

know that Jesus submitted himself to his heavenly Father's authority. Jesus certainly understood what it was to submit within the godhead, but as a human being this was something he had to learn in a practical and earthly sense. Obeying his Father as a human meant he would learn to live and grow under the authority of his parents in the beginning. Think about that for a second. Jesus had to obey Mary and Joseph. The Lord of creation, the King of kings, had to knuckle under and wash the dishes when Mom said to. Even when he was twelve and Joseph and Mary found him in the temple teaching the teachers, when his earthly parents said it was time to go, the text says that Jesus went and "continued to live in subjection" to them.

If you're a teen, don't let you're your mind gloss over it: Jesus went through his teen years, just like you, and had to learn to obey parents who, at times, must have seemed too strict. And he obeyed them anyway, because he knew it pleased his heavenly Father.

In obedience Jesus had to live a perfect life on earth, conduct the ministry that would change the world, die on the cross, and rise again. We know from his prayer in the Garden of Gethsemane that such obedience wasn't easy. In anguished and earnest supplication, Jesus said, "Father, if you are willing, take this cup from me; yet not my will, but yours be done" (Luke 22:42).

We also know that Jesus prayed frequently, especially in the morning, perhaps to get his marching orders for that day from his Father. When he was tempted in the wilderness by Satan (see Matthew 4:1–11), Jesus learned obedience by submitting himself to God's Word, not to what he might have preferred. Throughout his life Jesus obeyed every step of the way. In fact, he said in John 14:31, "The world must learn that I love the Father and that I do exactly what my Father has commanded me."

Ultimately Jesus learned obedience so that he could show us (1) that such complete obedience to the Father is possible; and (2) that we should imitate his example of total obedience to what the Bible, our leaders, our spirit, and our consciences tell us. It wasn't easy for Jesus, and it won't be easy for us. But it's possible, and it should be something we set our eyes on.

23

Jesus knew what it was like to LOSE someone he loved.

Joseph, the earthly father of Jesus, doesn't get much mileage in the New Testament. He's mentioned only a few times, notably in Matthew 1:18–25, where an angel appeared to him in a dream and assured him of Mary's fidelity: her pregnancy was of God, brought about by the Holy Spirit. The only other references to Joseph are in Matthew 2:13–23, where Joseph was warned by God to flee to protect the baby Jesus (which he did), and in Luke 2, where Joseph and Mary are taking Jesus to the temple for his circumcision and other rites.

Clearly, Joseph was a godly, committed follower of God who kept the Jewish religious rules and regulations. We also know from Matthew 13:55–56 that he was a carpenter. The people in Jesus's hometown remarked in disbelieving amazement, "Isn't this the carpenter's son? Isn't his mother's name Mary, and aren't his brothers James, Joseph, Simon and Judas? Aren't all his sisters with us?"

Besides these statements, we know nothing more of Joseph from the New Testament. What kind of man was he?

Matthew 1:19 says Joseph was a righteous man. Few people are given such a compliment in Scripture. To be called righteous was a high accolade that revealed an important truth about a person's character.

Joseph tried to do everything right: he followed the Law and lived justly and peaceably with his neighbors.

We also know from Matthew 1:19 that when Joseph became aware of Mary's pregnancy—apparently an act of infidelity, since he knew he was not the father—he "did not want to expose her to public disgrace," which would have been his right and a common response. Instead, "he had in mind to divorce her secretly." God knew how to pick the right people for his difficult assignments. Joseph's actions and attitudes show him to be a man of compassion, not vengeful or hasty to hurt others when he had been hurt.

Was Joseph much older than Mary, as some commentators have suggested? We don't know. But from the comments in Matthew 13, it seems likely he must have died before Jesus started his ministry. He wasn't present and is spoken about as if he were already dead. Some of the comments of church fathers in later writings say he was much older, but we don't know for certain.

Joseph helped raise Jesus, teaching him the skills of a carpenter. That takes a lot of working with a person, mentoring him, leading him, teaching him. Just because Jesus was God incarnate doesn't mean he always did everything perfectly the first time he tried to fashion a yoke or craft a chair. Joseph must have spent many hours with his son, guiding him in the work he knew well.

Undoubtedly Joseph taught Jesus the Scriptures when he was very young. Maybe he taught Jesus to respect and value women. He likely modeled kindness and compassion, provided protection and support, and encouraged Jesus to learn and grow. Perhaps he taught Jesus other important lessons in love, grief, letting go, and human suffering through his own death while Jesus was still a child or young man. If so, this is a lesson Jesus learned well. His compassion and empathy for those who suffered or faced loss was a hallmark of his ministry that sweetly mingled the earthly and the divine.

In a way, Joseph remains an enigma; but we can be sure that his life—and then his absence—were vital to Jesus's preparation and ministry. From all the men in all the world throughout all of history, God chose Joseph to be Jesus's teacher, protector, and example—his father. No matter how short his life or what else he accomplished, Joseph was a true success.

Undoubtedly, when Joseph died, Jesus grieved—whatever age he was. Jesus not only shows us his ability to grieve in John 11, with the death of Lazarus, but he experienced that emotion with his own earthly father. Did he weep at the sight of the still, lifeless body at the funeral, as I did when my grandfather died from a stroke when I was fourteen, leaving me feeling utterly bereft and confused and lost?

Did he go down to the river and throw rocks into the water, asking his heavenly Father, "Why?" as I did when my own father died of a heart attack at the age of sixty-seven?

Of course, Jesus was God in the flesh, so he probably saw things a bit differently than I did at the various times of loss in my life. But he was also completely human. He knows the hurt and pain we feel when we lose loved ones, even if we're deeply committed Christians and so were the deceased. Being a Christian doesn't mean you don't feel deep pain and grief at the death of a loved one.

But Jesus knows what that's like, and he knows how to comfort us in our darkness—as he did for me each time I've suffered such a loss, and as he will for you.

24

The carpenter's son grew up to be a SHEPHERD.

Sure, Jesus was a carpenter, like his earthly dad, Joseph. With few exceptions, boys in those days grew up to follow in their father's footsteps. But did you know Jesus grew up to be a shepherd too? Just like his heavenly Father. God is called a shepherd to his people (see Psalm 77:20, 78:71, 80:1).

Just like his Father, Jesus is described as our Shepherd in the New Testament. Three distinct shepherd titles are ascribed to Jesus, with unique and important implications. Let's look at them.

THE GOOD SHEPHERD

Jesus himself used this word picture when he said, "I am the good shepherd. The good shepherd lays down his life for the sheep. The hired hand is not the shepherd who owns the sheep. So when he sees the wolf coming, he abandons the sheep and runs away. Then the wolf attacks the flock and scatters it. The man runs away because he is a hired hand and cares nothing for the sheep. I am the good shepherd; I know my sheep and my sheep know me—just as the Father knows me and I know the Father—and I lay down my life for the sheep" (John 10:11–15).

The Good Shepherd is the sin-bearer, the one who lays down his life for the sheep. He is good: to Jews, "good" was the ultimate way of describing someone who was righteous, godly, and perfect. A good person was the penultimate signature of truth and godliness, so all these characteristics were wrapped up in the adjective *good*.

THE CHIEF SHEPHERD

In the Old and New Testaments, spiritual leaders (pastors) are often called shepherds (see Jeremiah 23:4; 1 Peter 5:2)—even incompetent and indifferent ministers, albeit they're called bad shepherds (see Ezekiel 34:2–10). In 1 Peter 5:1–4 Peter exhorted elders and pastors of God's flock to be exemplary, conscientious, and committed. He concluded, "When the Chief Shepherd appears, you will receive the crown of glory that will never fade away" (1 Peter 5:4). In this picture Jesus is the chief over all shepherds and ministers, pastors, leaders, and evangelists of the gospel who care for God's people. He is the one who gives rewards and crowns to those who have served well.

THE GREAT SHEPHERD

Finally, in Hebrews 13:20–21 we find one more reference to Jesus as a shepherd: "May the God of peace, who through the blood of the eternal covenant brought back from the dead our Lord Jesus, that great Shepherd of the sheep, equip you with everything good for doing his will."

This is the highest accolade of all: Jesus is the "great," or complete, shepherd in whom we find provision for every need. This Shepherd promises to give us everything we could possibly need to accomplish our tasks on earth and to move on to heaven.

Good. Chief. Great. What a fitting picture of Jesus as the ultimate Shepherd of those who love him.

25

No one knows what Jesus LOOKED like . . . on the outside.

The reflection in the mirror seems so important in our world today. It's the handsome and the beautiful who get noticed and the ugly and deformed who are pitied. Even our portraits of Jesus tend to display him as handsome and robust.

The Bible does describe the physical appearance of many people. Moses was said to be a beautiful child. People spoke of King Saul as being handsome, standing a head taller than anyone in Israel. David and Solomon were both "ruddy," handsome men.

But what of Jesus?

Nothing. Zilch. Zero. Not a word about a regal nose, handsome visage, or muscular body. In fact, the Bible tells us virtually nothing about Jesus's looks. Only that he "had no beauty or majesty to attract us to him, nothing in his appearance that we should desire him" (Isaiah 53:2).

From those words we might presume Jesus wasn't handsome, at least not in the way modern artists portray him. Apparently, in the mind of God, this was a nonissue. Jesus's words and character and love drew people to him, not his dashing good looks.

God tells us over and over: "What matters is who you are, not how you look." One good passage about how God feels about such things is found in 1 Samuel 16:7, when Samuel the prophet was sent to anoint a new king over Israel to replace the disobedient King Saul. God sent Samuel to the house of Jesse, a respectable man with eight sons. Jesse brought the eldest to him first, and Samuel thought Eliab was perfect for the king slot—handsome, strong, fearless. But God told the prophet, "Do not consider his appearance or his height, for I have rejected him. The LORD does not look at the things man looks at. Man looks at the outward appearance, but the LORD looks at the heart."

Jesse paraded seven of his sons in succession, but God chose none of them.

Samuel knew something was wrong, and he told Jesse that God had not chosen any of these men. Were these all of Jesse's sons?

Jesse admitted to having one more son, the youngest, but he just tended the sheep. The way it's written, it sounds as if it amazed even Jesse that anyone might notice his last son, David. But Samuel immediately ordered Jesse to bring the boy.

The Bible says David "was ruddy, with a fine appearance and handsome features" (1 Samuel 16:12). God said he was the one and ordered Samuel to anoint David the next king over Israel.

While David happened to be handsome, he was selected not for his looks but for his heart. Clearly, from what God said earlier to Samuel (that God does not look at a man's appearance but rather at his heart), this is the principle we should all adopt.

I think it was the heart of Jesus that moved people to follow him and, ultimately, die for him. When we read about him in the Bible, we don't see someone painted on the page. But we glimpse his character, his heart, his humanity, and compassion. That's what draws us to him. And those qualities are what will draw others to him through us.

26

Jesus chose some followers who seemed SLOW to catch on.

By the time John the Baptist began his God-ordained ministry of calling people to repentance and baptism, he was on the lookout for this Messiah, the One before whom he was to "make ready a people prepared for the Lord" (Luke 1:17). Multitudes went out to John at the Jordan River, and he baptized them for repentance from their sins and their commitment to look for the coming kingdom of God.

His ministry was so successful that the Jewish governing council, the Sanhedrin, sent a delegation to ask John if he was the Christ or Messiah ("anointed one") who was the promised Savior of the Jews and emancipator of the world. But John flatly denied it: "I am not the Christ" (John 1:20). He also denied being the prophet Elijah (who had never died and whose return was anticipated) or the prophet promised by Moses (Deuteronomy 18:15, 18). The only answer John would give to these questioners was to quote the prophet Isaiah: "I am the voice of one calling in the desert, 'Make straight the way for the Lord'" (John 1:23). John clearly saw himself as a fulfillment of prophecy and understood that his mission was to pave the way for the coming Messiah.

When Jesus finally did begin his own ministry, he came to be baptized by John. John objected, saying, "I need to be baptized by you, and do you come to me?" (Matthew 3:13). Clearly, John recognized

Jesus's preeminent position. But John consented to baptize Jesus when he replied, "Let it be so now; it is proper for us to do this to fulfill all righteousness" (Matthew 3:15).

As Jesus came up from the water, "heaven was opened" and the Spirit of God descended like a dove and lighted on Jesus. Then God's own voice spoke from heaven: "This is my Son, whom I love; with him I am well pleased" (Matthew 3:17).

Another gospel account quotes John as saying, "This is the one I meant when I said, 'A man who comes after me has surpassed me because he was before me'" (John 1:30). From these words we see that John accepted that this Lamb was far more important than he was and that Jesus possessed at least one divine quality, eternality: "He existed before me" (John 1:30 NASB). To say this was to equate Jesus with God the Father, because both existed before time began.

Perhaps John felt a little frustrated that people weren't heading off to follow Jesus, so he bore down a little harder, saying, "The one who sent me to baptize with water told me, 'The man on whom you see the Spirit come down and remain is he who will baptize with the Holy Spirit.' I have seen and I testify that this is the Son of God" (John 1:33–34).

John clearly wanted his followers to get the all-important message that the Messiah had come. "Get going after him!" was John's new message.

What more did people—especially John's disciples—need? They believed in John the Baptist enough to follow him into a life of asceticism in the desert; surely they would believe his witness that Jesus was the Son of God. They had been with John through months of his preparing the way for the Messiah, and now he had definitively pointed him out to them, yet none of them rushed to follow Jesus. It took until the next day, and one more push from John, for the first of them to be ready to take the plunge.

"Look, the Lamb of God!" John exclaimed when he saw Jesus. Then two of John's disciples, Andrew and probably John, the son of Zebedee, finally left John the Baptist and followed Jesus. Andrew came away convinced Jesus was the Messiah. He brought Jesus to his brother Simon, whom Jesus would give the nickname Peter, or Rocky. Andrew, Peter, and John all would be chosen by Jesus to be among his special Twelve, the disciples into whom Jesus would pour his life during his three-year ministry.

It's amazing when you consider all the evidence. Perhaps those people had seen Jesus be baptized, heard the voice from heaven, and listened as John boomed out his words about Jesus and pointed to him. Yet no one had followed right away. Why not?

Perhaps they were just too stunned. They knew John planned to point out the Messiah, but not today! They simply weren't ready.

Or maybe Jesus just didn't look the way they expected a Messiah to look. All we know about his appearance is that he "had no beauty or majesty to attract us to him" and was "despised and rejected by men" (Isaiah 53:2–3).

Throughout the Bible we see that God doesn't choose the handsome, the rich, or the movers and shakers of the world. No, he starts at the bottom with the poor, uneducated, down-and-out people, the ones who most need him.

Even today people remain slow to accept the truth about Jesus. How many friends and relatives do you have who obstinately reject your witness and that of others? The important thing is to follow John's example: keep telling them; keep speaking the truth; keep living the life. And keep praying that those you love will wake up to the truth and embrace the one who can make their lives beautiful.

27

Jesus passed God's test DURING Satan's temptations.

After Jesus's baptism, something surprising happened: "Jesus was led by the Spirit into the desert to be tempted by the devil" (Matthew 4:1). What was going on here? Was God leading Jesus into temptation? How can this be? It can't, as James wrote: "When tempted, no one should say, 'God is tempting me.' For God cannot be tempted by evil, nor does he tempt anyone" (James 1:13).

The question can be resolved when we understand the Greek word *peirasmos,* which can be translated "tempt" *or* "test." The fact is, God tests us, but Satan tempts us. So what's the difference?

God tests us to prove us, to allow us to demonstrate that we truly have faith and will obey him. And he also tests us to expose weaknesses so we can work to turn them into strengths.

On the other hand, Satan tempts us to give in to sin, fall into error, and possibly forsake our commitment to Christ. See the difference?

Jesus was "led" by the Spirit to a place where he would be "tested" by the Spirit and "tempted" by the devil. Perhaps God wanted to prove Jesus's integrity and veracity. But Satan's goal was to make Jesus sin and, consequently, be disqualified from his role as Savior of the world.

A similar idea is found in James 1:2–4, where the brother of Jesus wrote, "Consider it pure joy, my brothers, whenever you face trials of many kinds, because you know that the testing of your faith develops perseverance. Perseverance must finish its work so that you may be mature and complete, not lacking anything." We can face testing with genuine joy because we know what it produces: perseverance. That leads to maturity and completeness, to our becoming people who lack none of the skills needed for wise and godly living.

This was why Jesus was tested by the Spirit at the beginning of his ministry. He had to be proven not only acceptable and obedient but also prepared and worthy of the job he was sent to do. The Spirit had to make sure he could withstand the pain, pressure, and temptations Satan would throw at him all along the way. It also showed others that Jesus was ready for the work of ministry and the cross, the complex and difficult tasks God had given him.

This kind of testing happens to believers all the time. And James 1:12 tells us, "Blessed is the man who perseveres under trial, because when he has stood the test, he will receive the crown of life that God has promised to those who love him." Some of life's greatest happiness and joy come through persevering in trials. When we have faced the test and triumphed, we receive a special crown of life that God will give to all who pass the test and persevere.

28

Jesus aced his test by QUOTING from the Book.

Was Jesus ever really tempted to do something wrong? I mean *really* tempted? Feeling drawn, the whole body alive with the idea of the pleasure of doing the thing you know you shouldn't do? I believe he was.

The temptation of Jesus in the wilderness by Satan is recorded both in Matthew (4:1–11) and Luke (4:1–13). Let's look at the Matthew 4:1–11 passage.

Jesus had fasted for forty days and nights. Whether you think that's impossible or not, the truth is that it has been done by people living today, and it also had been accomplished by two Old Testament men: Moses (see Deuteronomy 9:9) and Elijah (see 1 Kings 19:8). Such fasting was even more a spiritual discipline than a physical one, and these prolonged periods of fasting often preceded some great event or new stage in a ministry or the life of the nation of Israel. Moses fasted forty days and nights while he was on Mount Sinai receiving the Law from God. Elijah also was about to receive an incredible revelation from God when he underwent his fast. Jesus's fast signaled the beginning of his earthly ministry.

When Matthew said Jesus was hungry after the forty days of fasting, he meant that Jesus was at the point of starvation. Physically he was at his weakest point. That's often when the enemy of our soul comes to us— and that's what happened with Jesus. Satan knew just how hungry Jesus was, and the first temptation centered on that need. Satan said, "If you are the Son of God, tell these stones to become bread" (Matthew 4:3). He was saying, "Since you say you're God's Son, why don't you prove it by meeting your own need right now? If you're capable of doing so, why not show it and maybe even save your own life while you're at it."

But Jesus would not eat until the temptation period was finished, because he had submitted himself to whatever his Father demanded. And he sure wasn't going to obey Satan. So he did what every person should do when facing a difficult test: he quoted from the Book: "Man does not live on bread alone but on every word that comes from the mouth of the LORD" (Deuteronomy 8:3).

The answer was spot on for Jesus's situation, but it's interesting to see the broader context of this quotation and how relevant it was to the temptation Jesus faced. Before entering the Promised Land, Moses told the people, "Remember how the LORD your God led you all the way in the desert these forty years, to humble you and to test you in order to know what was in your heart, whether or not you would keep his commands. He humbled you, causing you to hunger and then feeding you with manna, which neither you nor your fathers had known, to teach you that man does not live on bread alone" (Deuteronomy 8:2–3). Jesus was telling Satan that he would trust his Father to feed him when the time was right; but until then, he would live on God's Word.

Unable to make Jesus fail the first test, Satan tried another angle. He took Jesus to the pinnacle of the temple, which was built on a wall that extended deep into the Kidron Valley—a drop of some 450 feet. He then quoted Scripture himself, perhaps as if to say, "You wanna quote the Bible, Jesus? I can do that too."

"'If you are the Son of God,' he said, 'throw yourself down. For it is written: "He will command his angels concerning you, and they will lift you up in their hands, so that you will not strike your foot against a stone"'" (Matthew 4:6). This is actually a quote from Psalm 91:11–12. But Satan twisted its original meaning about trusting God and turned it into a taunt to test God. By jumping off and expecting God to save him at the last minute, Jesus would be testing God's worthiness and dependability. Did Jesus think God would pass that test, or not? If so, the devil goaded, prove it.

But Jesus didn't bite. Once again he returned to the book of Deuteronomy and countered, "It is also written: 'Do not test the Lord your God'" (Deuteronomy 6:16). In Deuteronomy 6 Moses was reminding the people of Israel about the time they ran out of water and demanded he give them something to drink. Moses correctly identified their complaining and demanding as putting the Lord to the test. To test God means to make a demand that he prove himself to you to show he is worthy of your trust. Jesus knew the thrust of Satan's taunt: to get him to do something to force God's hand to prove his Messiahship. But Jesus would have none of it.

Finally Satan took Jesus to a "very high mountain," where he could see all the great kingdoms of the world at one time. Presumably, Jesus could see such cities as Rome, Carthage, Babylon, Nineveh, Tyre, Sidon, Damascus, Alexandria, Antioch, and others. It must have been a glorious view. Next Satan claimed he owned these places and could give them to Jesus if he wanted. Satan's power over the world is supported by passages such as John 12:31; 14:30; 16:11; 2 Corinthians 4:4; and 1 John 5:19. He wasn't joking or bluffing about these places being under his power. Perhaps he really could have given them to Jesus—awarding him power, authority, and recognition without having to endure the suffering of the cross—if he would bow down and worship Satan.

Jesus shot back, "Away from me, Satan. For it is written, 'Worship the LORD your God and serve him only'" (Matthew 4:10). This is another quote from Deuteronomy (6:13–14). Bowing to Satan would have put Satan above Jesus and ruined God's plan to save the world.

Why did Jesus quote all three times from Deuteronomy? Perhaps because the passage is all about Israel's testing in the wilderness after Moses led them out of Egypt. It provided the perfect direction and inspiration because all of it was instruction on and good examples of how to pass any difficult test.

Jesus knew that all the answers were in God's Book. He had studied it, internalized it, and memorized it. He was prepared for any test. Are you?

29

Jesus knows what we're going through: he was TEMPTED as we are.

Hebrews 4:15 states it quite bluntly: "We do not have a high priest [Jesus] who is unable to sympathize with our weaknesses, but we have one who has been tempted in every way, just as we are—yet was without sin."

Is this possible? Was Jesus really tempted in every way?

Look at the record:

- *Fame:* Jesus was placed in a position of notoriety at his baptism. Might he have been tempted to use his fame for himself, or even to capitalize on it for his own comfort or pleasure?

- *The lust of the flesh, and the lust of the eyes, and the pride of life (1 John 2:16 KJV):* Satan's three temptations encouraged Jesus to (1) use his power to satisfy his own urges without permission from the Father; (2) gain fame by jumping off the temple and being rescued by God's angels; (3) become rich and have power over all the great cities of the world. Jesus wrestled with these temptations at the start of his ministry.

- *Being worshiped:* Jesus was worshiped by many people coming to him for help. Could this not have turned someone in his position into a megalomaniac?

- *Avoiding pain rather than doing God's will:* Jesus could do any miracle to help or save anyone; could he not have taken himself down from the cross and avoided that pain?

- *Sex:* Jesus worked with and knew many beautiful, rich, and powerful women. Could he not have succumbed to the lust of the flesh? Many other teachers and religious leaders have fallen for that one. Wouldn't it have been easy for someone in Jesus's place?

- *Gluttony and drunkenness:* He was even accused of this by the religious leaders who disapproved that he didn't share their ascetic lifestyle. Jesus associated with sinners of all stripes. Might this not have been a reasonable temptation?

- *Fortune:* couldn't Jesus have charged for his services or taken donations as many preachers do today?

- *Miracles:* could Jesus not have performed miracles just because he could, or done any number of crazy, wacky things just for attention?

- *Rejection:* couldn't Jesus have rejected his family or others who were slow to accept him and understand his identity and mission?

- *Hatred and prejudice:* couldn't Jesus have resorted to such emotional releases in confrontations with his enemies?

- *Cursing:* toward his enemies.

- *Violence:* against his enemies.

- *Unleashed anger:* against his enemies and anyone else who crossed him.

- *Revenge:* against his enemies.

Jesus undoubtedly faced other temptations too, but he never yielded. How is that possible? Because he was so filled with the Spirit of God and so closely in touch with God the Father that he would never go against them.

Jesus knows how to help us face similar temptations and triumph. 1 Corinthians 10:13 assures us he always will "provide a way out." Hebrews 4:14–16 tells us he was tempted in all the ways we are. So he's a good one to go to when we feel tempted by some powerfully attractive sin. Jesus can give us the power to resist—and show us the escape route. That's pretty strong comfort and support for all of us.

30

Jesus was PERFECT.

We know from many passages in the New Testament that Jesus was sinless (see Hebrews 4:14–16 and 2 Corinthians 5:21). To become the Savior of the world and pay for the sins of humanity, Jesus needed to be perfect, utterly without flaw, mistake, error, infraction, transgression, iniquity, or whatever you want to call it. Sin by any other name is still sin. And the people who gave us the New Testament clearly portrayed Jesus as unblemished and without such a problem.

Consider for a moment what it took to live up to the claim of perfection. Jesus had to maintain a perfect record of never lying, stealing, cheating, fornicating, or coveting. He never even had an evil or lustful thought. Hatred? Not once, at least of a specific person. Prejudice? Nope. Bias? Covering up something? Gambling? Getting drunk? Doing drugs? Never. Not one slip of the tongue. Never a single nasty word. He was perfect in every sense. No one could accuse him of any crime. The accusations the Pharisees and Sadducees ultimately brought to Jesus's trials before Pilate, Annas, and Herod all evaporated quickly when the facts came out. Pilate actually found him not guilty of anything but crucified him anyway because it was too much trouble to let him go free.

But think of the ramifications of this idea. How careful did Jesus have to be? How cautious? How plodding? How never daring to rustle a feather?

That's the strange thing. When you meet the Jesus of the New Testament, you never get the idea that he was being careful not to do anything wrong. You never sense that he was cautious or calculated about what he said, like today's public figures are when interviewed. Jesus always seems natural, normal, and utterly without a pose. He didn't fake it at all. He was the real thing.

How did he pull this off? One way: the Spirit of God so filled and led and controlled him that he always did God's will—happily, freely, nonchalantly, and without pretense. And all the time he never griped or protested or whined. He enjoyed pleasing his Father, and he just went about his business day by day without ever sinning.

It's astonishing, when you think about it. Didn't he long to react sometime to some pompous person with sarcastic or barbed wit? Didn't Jesus ever just want to launch a fist into some Pharisee's self-righteous jaw? Did he not notice the pretty women who tried to catch his eye?

If Jesus had made one single error, if he had put down one person unrighteously, if he had reacted in anger to even one of the multitude of insults hurled at him, he would have been disqualified as Savior of the world. Once. Just once. That's all it would have taken.

And yet he pulled off this sinless-life thing without a hitch, without even seeming stilted or overly concerned or even the slightest bit strained.

Frankly, I don't know how he did it, even with the Holy Spirit. But you know what? One day we'll be just like him in that respect—sinless. Going through our days always doing right and good, without hesitation or having to think about it. We'll be awarded crowns of righteousness. And we won't even be proud about the accomplishment.

31

Jesus's NEIGHBORS tried to throw him off a cliff.

It only makes sense to establish your base in familiar territory. For Jesus this would have been Nazareth. That was where his parents had settled after returning from Egypt when the threat from King Herod ended. But when Jesus began his ministry, after being baptized by John in the Jordan River, he promptly left Nazareth and moved to a new location—to Capernaum, which was by the Sea of Galilee. Why the change?

In Luke 4 we learn that Jesus first began to minister in Galilee, preaching and healing. But when he returned to Nazareth and stood in the synagogue to teach, the rabbi handed him the scroll of the prophet Isaiah. Jesus undoubtedly knew it well, and he turned immediately to the following passage and read: "The Spirit of the Lord is on me, because he has anointed me to preach good news to the poor. He has sent me to proclaim freedom for the prisoners and recovery of sight for the blind, to release the oppressed, to proclaim the year of the Lord's favor" (Luke 4:18–19). The people knew this passage well too, for it was often cited as a primary text for the coming of the Messiah.

Jesus rolled up the scroll, gave it back to the attendant, and sat down to teach. "Today this scripture is fulfilled in your hearing" (Luke 4:21), he told the attentive audience.

No one got upset at that point, but they probably pinched themselves a bit: Jesus had just told them he was the Messiah. Luke described the mixed audience reaction: "All spoke well of him and were amazed at the gracious words that came from his lips" (Luke 4:22). But there were also some questions: "'Isn't this Joseph's son?' they asked" (Luke 4:22). In other words, "How could a hometown boy, little Jesus—the carpenter's kid—possibly be the Messiah we've awaited for thousands of years?"

Perhaps knowing their incredulity, Jesus said, "Surely you will quote this proverb to me: 'Physician, heal yourself! Do here in your hometown what we have heard that you did in Capernaum.' I tell you the truth," he continued, "no prophet is accepted in his hometown. I assure you that there were many widows in Israel in Elijah's time, when the sky was shut for three and a half years and there was a severe famine throughout the land. Yet Elijah was not sent to any of them, but to a widow in Zarephath in the region of Sidon. And there were many in Israel with leprosy in the time of Elisha the prophet, yet not one of them was cleansed—only Naaman the Syrian" (Luke 4:23–27).

This ignited the crowd. Jesus was basically saying, "I know you turned out today because you wanted to see me do the miracles you've heard so much about, but I'm not going to put on a show to prove to you who I am. You people are just as unbelieving as the people in the days of Elijah, when King Ahab and Jezebel (two of the worst idolators in Israel's history) ruled. God couldn't find anybody worthy of helping except those two Gentiles."

Nothing disturbed Jews more than being told Gentiles were more to God's liking than they were. So, as Luke tells us, "All the people in the synagogue were furious when they heard this. They got up, drove him out of the town, and took him to the brow of the hill on which the town was built, in order to throw him down the cliff. But he walked right through the crowd and went on his way" (Luke 4:28–30).

After that kind of reception, who wouldn't leave?

I remember well the first days after my conversion. Excitement pulsed through me like a geyser. I told all my friends what had happened. "I met God." "Jesus is real." "You've got to know him." Some were intrigued, and two of them later became Christians, both remaining steadfast to this day. But others, including some family members, fought, argued, and in some cases just wrote me off as a fanatic.

Many new Christians encounter a similar polarizing and wonder what they've done wrong. The answer is, probably nothing. Maybe their enthusiasm was a little overpowering. Or maybe their preaching felt to the hearers a little like judging. In those cases words laced with love, compassion, and straightforward honesty may go a long way in mending things. On the other hand, we have to realize that to some extent, others' reactions are just part of the package. If they've rejected Jesus, so they will eventually reject you.

What did Jesus do about this monumental rejection? He went to Capernaum, where he recruited several of his disciples—Peter, Andrew, John, James, and Matthew the tax collector. By going to Capernaum Jesus also fulfilled prophecy from Isaiah 9:1–2. Matthew repeated the prophecy in relation to how Jesus fulfilled it: "Land of Zebulun and land of Naphtali, the way to the sea, along the Jordan, Galilee of the Gentiles—the people living in darkness have seen a great light; on those living in the land of the shadow of death a light has dawned" (Matthew 4:15–16).

Whatever people's reactions, Jesus carried on with doing God's will. And so should we.

32

Jesus used UNUSUAL methods and criteria in choosing his disciples.

You know Peter, James and John, Philip and Andrew, and Judas Iscariot. Do you know the names of the rest of Jesus's twelve disciples? They were Nathanael (also known as Bartholomew), Thomas, Matthew (also called Levi), James the son of Alphaeus (or James the Less), Simon the Zealot or Canaanite, and Judas the brother of James (sometimes called Thaddaeus). According to John 1, John the Baptist pointed out Jesus to Andrew and another follower, and Andrew spent the whole day with the Lord, probably asking every question under the sun.

Then Andrew went and found his brother Simon. "We have found the Messiah!" he told him, and brought him to Jesus. Jesus seemed to truly know Simon. He looked at him and said, "You are Simon son of John. You will be called Cephas." *Cephas* is translated "Peter" and means "rock." Maybe he was the first Rocky. Will anyone make a movie about that one?

The next day Jesus found Philip and exhorted him, "Follow me" (John 1:43). Philip did so, then promptly went off to find Nathanael and share his good news: "We have found the one Moses wrote about in the Law, and about whom the prophets also wrote—Jesus of Nazareth, the son of Joseph" (John 1:45). To which Nathanael, unconvinced, replied: "Nazareth! Can anything good come from there?" (John 1:46). As we've seen before, Nazareth had a bad reputation. The notion that something good—especially spiritually—could come from Nazareth would have shocked any good Jew. But Philip responded simply, "Come and see" (John 1:46).

Once again Jesus seemed to look into a person and see his soul. He said of Nathanael, "Here is a true Israelite, in whom there is nothing false" (John 1:47).

Obviously surprised at Jesus's unexpected insight, Nathanael asked, "How do you know me?" (John 1:48).

Jesus's answer was even more unnerving: "I saw you while you were still under the fig tree before Philip called you" (John 1:48).

What was Nathanael doing under the fig tree? We don't know. Maybe he was praying about the Messiah. Perhaps Nathanael had been asking God to lead him to the Messiah. Whatever the case, instantly Nathanael was convinced that something good had indeed come out of Nazareth. "Then Nathanael declared, 'Rabbi, you are the Son of God; you are the King of Israel'" (John 1:49).

Jesus said, "You believe because I told you I saw you under the fig tree. You shall see greater things than that" (John 1:50). What Jesus said came true. As a disciple, Nathanael witnessed many miracles.

Jesus called Peter and Andrew, then James and John from their fishing boats (see Mark 1:14–20). "Come follow me," Jesus said, "and I will make you fishers of men" (Mark 1:17). He called Matthew from his tax collector's booth (Matthew 9:9). As for the other disciples, the Bible doesn't give us the details of how they were called.

But did you know that Jesus had more than just these twelve disciples? Actually, he had more than seventy-two disciples (plus the Twelve) for this is the number he sent out to minister in his name (see Luke 10:1–2).

Though it's clear that Jesus had many disciples following him, at some point he went up on a mountain alone and spent the whole night in prayer, discussing with his Father whom he should select to be his closest companions. These would be with him constantly and would enjoy a special relationship as students and friends. They would have to leave all and follow him with commitment and total devotion.

Jesus used UNUSUAL methods

After that night on the mountain, Jesus called his disciples to him and chose twelve of them, whom he also designated apostles (see Luke 6:12–16).

What do we know about these men? Peter, Andrew, James, and John were fishermen. Matthew was a tax collector. Philip appeared to be some kind of accountant or someone who worked with money. Simon was a Zealot, one of the rebel groups seeking to overthrow Rome. Of the others we know little to nothing. Many of them are never quoted in the Gospels.

In choosing these disciples, Jesus seemed to go for certain characteristics:

- Simple and humble over sophisticated and worldly

- Business-type people rather than the religious class (such as Pharisees)

- Nonleaders rather than leaders (such as the Sadducees)

- Nonteachers

- Unpolished and plainspoken; uneducated

- Some could read and write; we don't know about others.

What did they have to do to be considered for the role of disciple? They had to leave everything and follow Jesus.

Nothing else.

It was an awesome responsibility to accept. Many of these men were married and had families. But for them, somehow the question was not "Why should I?" but "Why wouldn't I?"

If you had lived then, could you have been one of Jesus's disciples?

33

Jesus was a great FISHING guide.

You probably know that some of Jesus's disciples were fishermen—Peter, Andrew, James, and John. They did a thriving business on the shores of Lake Galilee and would become devoted followers of Jesus.

But did you know that Jesus was quite the fisherman himself? We're not told that he was good with a net or anything like that. No, Jesus fished strictly by instinct and with miraculous power. Look at two situations where he managed to fill the boats to overflowing.

Luke 5:1–11 tells us that early in Jesus's ministry, he taught by the sea. Crowds pressed in on him until it was time to try something new: he got into Simon's fishing boat, they pushed out a short distance from the shore, and Jesus taught crowds on the shore while sitting in the boat. If you've ever been on the water and noticed how well sound travels, you'll understand how this helped amplify Jesus's voice so more people than ever could hear him clearly. When he finished the talk, he told Simon, "Put out into deep water, and let down the nets for a catch" (Luke 5:4).

Simon, apparently not much impressed with Jesus's fly-tying strategy, protested: "Master, we've worked hard all night and haven't caught anything. But because you say so, I will let down the nets" (Luke 5:5). Simon didn't object too much. Perhaps he was just polite. (Simon Peter?!) He thought Jesus was a good teacher and had probably already had the encounter mentioned in John 1, where Jesus changed his name to Rocky (Peter). But Peter knew fish, and the best time to catch them was at night. Perhaps to humor Jesus, maybe out of respect for him and his teaching, he decided to do as Jesus said.

They headed deeper, let out the nets, and immediately caught so many fish that the nets began to break. They signaled to their partners in another boat, and soon both boats were so full of fish that they began to sink.

Mighty miracle or beginner's luck? Simon Peter never even considered the possibility of luck. Struck once more by Jesus's awesome power, he fell at the Lord's knees, and cried, "Go away from me, Lord; I am a sinful man" (Luke 5:8). When confronted with the power and holiness of God, finite, sinful humanity recognizes its unworthiness. Simon knew he wasn't worthy to be in the same boat as Jesus, much less the recipient of this largesse—he was just an ordinary, sinful, inadequate man. But Jesus kindly reassured him: "Don't be afraid; from now on you will catch men" (Luke 5:10). So they (likely Simon, Andrew, James, and John) pulled their boats out of the water, left everything—boats, nets, gear—and followed Jesus. Full time. Forever. That was the official start of their discipleship.

The second occasion clinched Jesus's status as all-time greatest fishing guide. Shortly after Jesus's death and resurrection, several disciples followed Peter's lead and went fishing (see John 21:1–9). Perhaps they didn't know what to do without Jesus being with them. They were still trying to figure out exactly what had happened with Jesus's death and resurrection; still trying to determine what it was they should do next. When you're confused, scared, and worried, it can be a relief to do something you're familiar with and that won't tax your brain too heavily. Seven of them fished all night but caught nothing.

Early the next morning Jesus stood on shore and called to them, "Friends, haven't you any fish?" (John 21:5).

They didn't recognize Jesus, so they just said, "No."

"Throw your net on the right side of the boat and you will find some," Jesus instructed them (John 21:6).

That's kind of remarkable. When it comes to boats and water, does it really matter much which side of the boat you're fishing from? But that's the beauty of it, for when they obeyed, they caught so many fish—153 of them—that they were unable to haul the net back into the boat.

Immediately John said, "It is the Lord!" (John 21:7). Peter wrapped himself in his outer garment, dove overboard, and swam in, about a hundred yards. When everyone got to shore, they found Jesus tending a fire with some fish and bread roasting over it. Jesus served them all breakfast, adding several of the fish they'd just caught to the menu.

What's amazing about these stories is that they're like bookends. The first happened at the beginning of Jesus's ministry, the second at the end. It's as if the Lord were completely closing the chapter of the disciples' fishing days. He had shown them how they could, if they wanted, with his assistance, have the greatest fishing business on earth. But that was not his purpose or theirs. They would soon be fishing for men, and that was what Jesus meant to show them. It was as if he were saying, "If it's fish you want, that's easy. Just put down your nets where and when I say so. But if you want something much bigger and greater—people, eternal souls—then come with me. I'll be your guide on the greatest, most fulfilling adventure you could ever hope for. I'll show you how to do that too."

34

Demons PUBLICLY revealed Jesus's secret identity.

The disciples often didn't get it. In spite of inspired glimpses from time to time, they never really seemed to totally get who Jesus was until after he rose from the dead and appeared to them. Some might even say they didn't *really* get it until Pentecost, when the Holy Spirit came into them and opened their minds to the truth. Some gained inklings of this truth along the way—like Nathanael in John 1:44–51 and Peter in his great declaration about Jesus being "the Christ" in Matthew 16:13–17. But for many it wasn't until the Spirit really "opened" their eyes that they could truly "see."

The chief priests and Pharisees grasped that Jesus claimed to be the Messiah, but they thought he was an impostor and, therefore, had committed blasphemy. They crucified him for it.

Even Jesus's own family didn't seem to get it until after his crucifixion.

But one group did get it from the start, and you would think they'd be precisely the ones who would try to hide it. But apparently they screamed his identity out every chance they got. Who were they? The demons Jesus cast out.

The first such instance is recorded in Mark 1:21–28. Jesus had been teaching in the synagogue in Capernaum on the Sabbath. Apparently he was having quite an impact. "The people were amazed at his teaching, because he taught them as one who had authority, not as the teachers of the law" (Mark 1:22). But then a man from among those in the synagogue, who was possessed by an evil spirit, cried out, "What do you want with us, Jesus of Nazareth? Have you come to destroy us? I know who you are—the Holy One of God!" (Mark 1:24).

"'Be quiet!' said Jesus sternly. 'Come out of him!' The evil spirit shook the man violently and came out of him with a shriek" (Mark 1:25–26).

It was clear Jesus was more powerful than the demon, and it was also clear that Jesus didn't like demons telling the world who he was.

Similar incidents are recorded in Mark 3:7–12; 5:1–17. The amazing thing is that these demons recognized and cried out the fact that Jesus was the Son of God.

Why did they do this? It might have been a lame attempt to discredit Jesus in the eyes of the people. In fact, just a few verses later, in Mark 3:22, we see the "teachers of the Law" claiming that Jesus was "possessed by Beelzebub. By the prince of demons he is driving out demons."

Why did Jesus react to it so strongly? Perhaps because it was not yet time for the revelation of who he was. And certainly that pronouncement of great truth was not for the demons to make.

35

Jesus couldn't stop PEOPLE from talking.

Believe me, if I ever healed someone or raised someone from the dead, you can be sure I would expect some fanfare, some praise, and a few pats on the back—maybe a book contract or two.

Not Jesus. Quite often he told people not to tell anyone about what he'd just done. But many of them, understandably perhaps, just couldn't keep their mouths shut and told anyway. Why might Jesus have told people not to tell about their healings? Look at the following passages.

In Mark 1:40–45 we read that Jesus healed a leper who came to him. The moment the man was healed, Jesus said, "See that you don't tell this to anyone" (Mark 1:44). Jesus might have had several reasons for this. For one thing, his message was more important than his miracles. Miracles lent authority to his ministry, showed his compassion, and also confirmed his deity. But without the message, a miracle only fixed a temporary problem. One day the person would die, and then what? If the miracle didn't point the person to the message and the message to faith and redemption, what good was it?

A second reason might have been related to Jesus's concern about his enemies. If the miracle got reported to everyone, the people who hated him could find him and possibly provide further problems for his ministry. It's also likely that though Jesus was not afraid of being killed "before his time," he didn't want his ministry to proceed at too fast a rate. He needed to train his disciples, and that took time. If others marauded him constantly about healing and other needs, he would never have time to minister to the Twelve.

In spite of the debt of gratitude the man owed Jesus, he disobeyed his instruction. "Instead he went out and began to talk freely, spreading the news" (Mark 1:45). The consequence of this breach? "As a result, Jesus could no longer enter a town openly, but stayed outside in lonely places. Yet the people still came to him from everywhere" (Mark 1:45). Too much exposure about the miracles Jesus did ended up actually hindering his ministry and hurting those he might otherwise have helped. If you were a lame or blind person who couldn't go outside the city, your access to Jesus had just been effectively cut off.

A third factor could have been that Jesus didn't want to be besieged by people seeking miracles at the expense of his message. It wasn't that he didn't want to heal; he healed everyone who ever came to him, and he healed some who never asked for it. But he needed quiet to speak, and a raucous crowd, whooping it up over each example of spiritual power, would have made that impossible.

A fourth possible reason involved the good of the leper himself: perhaps Jesus didn't want him to become a source of curiosity, or worse, a sensation. This could have badly damaged the leper, who, having been ostracized from society for so many years, would have obviously enjoyed the treatment—until he was confronted by unbelievers and ridiculed as an idiot, as happened in other instances (see the healing of the blind man in John 9:13–34).

In Matthew 9:27–31 we see another example of Jesus telling those he healed to keep it to themselves. Inside, away from the scrutiny of the crowd, Jesus healed two blind men, then warned them sternly, "See that no one knows about this" (Matthew 9:30). But like the leper, they couldn't seem to contain themselves. "They went out and spread the news about him all over that region" (Matthew 9:31).

Matthew 12:15–21 shows yet another example of Jesus telling those he healed to keep quiet—this time about who he was. Aware that the

Pharisees were trying to kill him for healing a man on the Sabbath, Jesus withdrew, but "many followed him, and he healed all their sick, warning them not to tell who he was" (Matthew 12:15–16). Matthew also quoted Isaiah 42:1–4 in giving us an idea of why Jesus wanted to keep people from sensationalizing his ministry: "Here is my servant whom I have chosen, the one I love, in whom I delight; I will put my Spirit on him, and he will proclaim justice to the nations. He will not quarrel or cry out; no one will hear his voice in the streets. A bruised reed he will not break, and a smoldering wick he will not snuff out, till he leads justice to victory" (Matthew 12:18–20). Jesus was gentle and quiet. His ministry was not to be a spectacle; but people just couldn't keep their tongues from wagging.

36

Jesus EMBRACED sinners.

Was Jesus some hard-nosed guy who went around pointing out everyone's faults? Was he the ultimate confronter—a person who spoke freely and honestly but also directly and accusingly?

Strangely enough, in the Gospels we rarely find Jesus "confronting" anyone about sin. In Mark 2:5 he told a paralytic, "Son, your sins are forgiven," but he didn't point out any of them. In John 5:14 he told an invalid he'd just healed, "See, you are well again. Stop sinning or something worse may happen to you." What the sin was, we do not know. Jesus rarely revealed such personal and distressing details where anyone else might hear, gawk, or pass judgment.

When the Pharisees and scribes asked his disciples why he ate and drank with tax collectors and sinners, Jesus replied, "It is not the healthy who need a doctor, but the sick. But go and learn what this means: 'I desire mercy, not sacrifice.' For I have not come to call the righteous, but sinners" (Matthew 9:12–13).

In Matthew 23:1–39 Jesus blasted the teachers of the Law and the Pharisees, saying, "Everything they do is done for men to see" (Matthew 23:5). "Woe to you, teachers of the Law and Pharisees, you hypocrites! You shut the kingdom of heaven in men's faces. You yourselves do not enter, nor will you let those enter who are trying to" (Matthew 23:13). The whole chapter is one specific condemnation after another.

But this was characteristic of Jesus. He spoke bluntly and sharply with the leaders, teachers of the Law, and Pharisees, the people who best knew the Law, and assaulted them verbally for their hypocrisy. But to the average man or woman, the disciple and follower, Jesus was unswervingly gentle and compassionate. He never judged or condemned them but instead kindly told them to repent and walk the narrow way. He invited them to come with him and learn how. And he never berated them for their missteps and mistakes.

Perhaps the greatest example of this is his treatment of Peter. Jesus warned Peter that he would deny him. But it wasn't a harsh, judgmental statement; it was filled with compassion and empathy. Read Luke 22:31–34. You can almost hear the kindness in Jesus's words.

Then notice how Jesus spoke to Peter afterward, during one of his resurrection appearances (see John 21). Jesus had a conversation with Peter in which he asked the disciple three times, "Do you love me?" Peter replied three times that he did, and each time Jesus replied with: "Feed my lambs," "Take care of my sheep," or "Feed my sheep." No reminding Peter of his failure: he didn't have to. They both knew what had happened, and Jesus understood that Peter was truly sorry and had repented. Jesus asked the question three times, perhaps because of the three times Peter denied Jesus. But everything Jesus did and said to Peter was gentle and kind, not at all accusing.

Jesus was the consummate leader. He was always hard on himself but soft and loving with those who recognized their failures and repented. His dealings with the humble and repentant were memorable for their gentility and compassion. Only those who refused to acknowledge their sin and who willfully defied God were confronted with judgment. The choice was always up to the individual—just as it is today.

37

Jesus brought CHANGE to the tax collectors.

What does a wealthy tax collector seem to need more than anything else? Change! When you understand the business practices and ethics of most tax collectors in Bible times, you'll understand their need for change. And you probably won't be surprised to see that Jesus was the one who gave at least a couple of tax collectors exactly what they needed.

Tax collectors were despised in Israel. They were outcasts, expelled from the synagogue and excluded from serving as witnesses and judges because they were considered morally unacceptable. Jews considered them traitors because they paid the Romans for the right to tax their own people—and, of course, keep a chunk of the money for themselves. The Roman government dictated how much money they required, but tax collectors frequently charged people much higher rates and pocketed the extra. No wonder they often became exceedingly wealthy—and were hated. These men were often hard-bitten and tough, and many probably cared little what anyone thought or said about them.

Yet in the Gospels we're shown two tax collectors who changed. They came to love and follow Jesus. The first is Matthew, or Levi, who wrote the book of Matthew and was one of Jesus's twelve disciples. Jesus trusted and loved him. Matthew was sitting at a tax collector's booth—likely a sort of tollbooth on a major road—when Jesus called him. According to

Matthew 9:9 Matthew didn't hesitate at all but left everything behind—his lucrative position, his opportunity for advancement, and his tarnished reputation—and followed Jesus. That's really about all that we know about this godly man who wrote the first Gospel, but just think about the change. From reviled, ethically challenged tax collector to follower of Christ, apostle, gospel writer, changer of the world. That's quite an improvement.

A second tax collector to whom Jesus brought change was Zacchaeus (see Luke 19:1–10). Zacchaeus was not just any tax collector; he was a chief tax collector of an especially prosperous region. No wonder he was wealthy. When Jesus passed through Jericho, Zacchaeus wanted to see who this famous person was. He stationed himself along the route so he could see Jesus, but being short, he couldn't see over the crowd that had gathered. Probably not accustomed to being denied anything he wanted, Zacchaeus climbed a sycamore-fig tree so he could see over the crowd. "When Jesus reached the spot, he looked up and said to him, 'Zacchaeus, come down immediately. I must stay at your house today'" (Luke 19:5).

How did Jesus see the man? How did he know his name? Obviously Jesus knew Zacchaeus's heart, even as he knew his occupation. In spite of the social injunction against associating with ostracized tax collectors, Jesus spoke directly to this one and invited himself to the man's house—a social faux pas on many levels. But for Zacchaeus it must have been like cool water to a man dying in the desert. Someone acknowledged him, called out to him by name, may even have smiled at him, looked him in the eye, and willingly reached out in fellowship.

Zacchaeus clambered down out of the tree and gladly welcomed Jesus to his house. Many in the crowd grumbled about whom Jesus had chosen to associate with. But this was nothing new. Jesus had done this many times before. Maybe that's because his purpose in going to Zacchaeus's house—or to anyone's house—wasn't for good food or to increase his social standing but to bring redemption and change. That's what he brought to Zacchaeus's house that day.

The change was evident in Zacchaeus's announcement: "Look, Lord! Here and now I give half of my possessions to the poor, and if I have cheated anybody out of anything, I will pay back four times the amount."

Why four times the amount? The Law required that a person give one-fifth as restitution for fraud (plus the original amount), according to Numbers 5:6–7. "Four times" restitution was required only in the case of stealing and killing sheep (see Exodus 22:1). Perhaps Zacchaeus saw his sin as requiring the maximum penalty under the Law to show his true conviction and repentance. It seems likely the generosity of Zacchaeus's offer reflected the vast size of the change wrought in his heart.

What can we make of the stories of these two tax collectors? Jesus Christ changes people. On the spot. Without reservation. When a person becomes a true Christian, real change takes place in the heart. He becomes a different person, a "new creation" (2 Corinthians 5:17). And that makes all the difference.

Need change?

38

Jesus violated the laws of his day, but NOT God's laws.

The religious leaders' opposition to Jesus started with the Sabbath. The seventh day of the week was to be a day of rest (Sabbath means "rest" or "desist"). When God gave Moses the Ten Commandments, the fourth one focused on this. God said, "Remember the Sabbath day by keeping it holy. Six days you shall labor and do all your work, but the seventh day is a Sabbath to the LORD your God. On it you shall not do any work" (Exodus 20:8–10).

That was God's law. But the Jewish leaders had created all kinds of little laws about the Sabbath—man-made laws—that were meant to help people not break the Sabbath. For instance, one rule contended that you could not walk on grass on the Sabbath. Why? Because you might dislodge a seed, plant it, and thus be guilty of planting and working on the Sabbath. Another one concerned spitting: you couldn't spit on the Sabbath, because someone might come along, step on the spit, leave a little furrow in the soil, and thus be "plowing," which was another form of work. A woman couldn't look into a mirror on the Sabbath because she might notice a gray hair, pluck it out, and perform more work.

Thousands of these little rules had been added by generations of rabbis who probably just wanted to keep the Sabbath day holy. The problem was that many Jews also found ways to skirt the issue of the Sabbath when something became inconvenient. For instance, one of the Sabbath rules stipulated you couldn't travel more than one mile from your home on that day. However, wherever you had any possessions—maybe you left a toothpick sticking up in a field, or you took off a sock and dropped it there by the side of the road—that was considered your home too.

Knowing this detail, some Jews took advantage of it. If they wanted to make a journey of more than a mile on the Sabbath, they would simply send a servant out along the route to drop some possession every mile. Thus, a supposedly God-fearing Jew could make the desired trip on the Sabbath without violating the commandment.

All kinds of ways were devised to get around the "no work at all" restrictions of the Sabbath commandment. This obeying the letter of the law while ignoring its spirit was one reason Jesus called the religious leaders hypocrites. He infuriated them because he didn't cite any sticky rules to justify healing on the Sabbath; he just did it. He challenged the authorities and their heartless rules every step of the way as he faithfully fulfilled God's higher laws of love, mercy, and compassion. Their tendency to major in legalistic, minor points of the law while totally ignoring the more important matters would later be described by Jesus as straining out gnats while swallowing camels (see Matthew 23:24).

Jesus confronted the Pharisees' beliefs head on and boldly continued doing good on the Sabbath, such as healing and casting out demons. He also defended his disciples against accusations they'd violated the Sabbath by going into the grain fields and picking heads of grain to eat when they were hungry (see Matthew 12:1–8). He gave three examples of acceptable lawbreaking to underscore that human need, mercy, and compassion superseded the strictest adherence to the letter of the law. He reminded them of David's taking the consecrated bread that was only to be eaten by priests to show that even God's laws were flexible when it came down to legitimate physical needs of people. Stopping suffering supersedes Sabbath law.

Jesus then reminded the Pharisees that even the priests break the Sabbath every week when they serve in the temple, and yet they are considered innocent. Serving God supersedes Sabbath law. And finally he appealed directly to the Pharisees: "If any of you has a sheep and it falls into a pit on the Sabbath, will you not take hold of it and lift it out? How much more valuable is a man than a sheep! Therefore it is lawful to do good on the Sabbath" (Matthew 12:11–12). Saving someone supersedes Sabbath law.

Jesus summed up the entire lesson with these words: "If you had known what these words mean, 'I desire mercy, not sacrifice,' you would not have condemned the innocent. For the Son of Man is Lord of the Sabbath" (Matthew 12:7–8). As God, Jesus was the one who created the Sabbath in the first place, so he surely knew what he should or should not do on that day. He would keep God's Sabbath laws by doing good—even if it meant breaking the Pharisees' meanspirited laws.

After several confrontations over Jesus's so-called violations of the Sabbath, the New Testament tells us that the Jews conspired to kill him. This, despite the fact that the sixth commandment is, "You shall not murder" (Exodus 20:13).

Keeping the "spirit of the Law" is more difficult than following some list of things you think will make God sit up and take notice of you. Over and over we find in Jesus's teaching that the spirit of the Law is love—toward God and toward humankind. "Love," the apostle Paul wrote, "is the fulfillment of the law" (Romans 13:10).

39

Jesus was God in the FLESH.

What was the greatest controversy of Jesus's time? His identity. Who was he—man or God or both? Did he really have power to forgive sins? Wasn't that God's province alone? And was he the one prophesied for centuries in the Old Testament who would "preach good news to the poor. . . . bind up the brokenhearted . . . proclaim freedom for the captives and release from darkness for the prisoners"(Isaiah 61:1)? The Jews wanted—no, longed for—the Messiah. But what they expected was a political Messiah, someone who would break the bonds of the Roman Empire, give everyone a multitude of financial and physical blessings (that condo in Jerusalem, that vacation to Rome), and in general make everything hunky-dory—especially for the leaders of the Jews, who were certainly the most worthy of all this largesse.

What they got was Jesus—humble, caring, gentle. A healer of sick people—lepers, demon-possessed, blind, and lame. And a person who had little or nothing to say about Rome, empires, Caesars, or taxes. Jesus just didn't fill the bill. Rather than advocating revolution—or at least resisting the hated Roman occupation—Jesus told his disciples, "If someone strikes you on the right cheek, turn to him the other also. And if someone wants to sue you and take your tunic, let him have your cloak as well. If someone forces you to go one mile, go with him two miles" (Matthew 5:39–41). He counseled patience, civility, kindness, goodness, and godliness, of all things. He preached about sins people actually committed. He called for repentance from everyone, not just the tax collectors, prostitutes, and rogues. And he seemed to save his most incendiary railings for the Pharisees, Sadducees, and scribes—the very people whom God surely considered the cream of the crop. But Jesus called them hypocrites and vipers.

So when Jesus started making claims about being God, it made them livid. ("I Am" was the name by which God revealed himself to the Israelites in Exodus 3:14, a name so holy that Jewish leaders refused even to speak it. Yet Jesus repeatedly used this phrase to refer to himself—"I am the bread of life," "I am the Way, the Truth, and the Life," "I am"—and the Pharisees knew what Jesus meant by it.) They just wouldn't take it.

In fact, for a long time Jesus tried to keep his identity quiet. When he made these kinds of revelations to his closest disciples or someone he healed, he often followed it up with a caveat: "Don't tell anyone about this."

But why tell people to keep quiet about the most stupendous, incredible, world-shaking thing that had happened in their lifetime—that God had come down into human flesh and lived among them like a typical man? Because it wasn't yet Jesus's time to die: his ministry was not yet complete. And he knew how the jealous religious leaders would react—precisely the way they did: they sought to kill him.

You see, Jesus's identity was the stick that broke the camel's back for the people who most wanted him gone (see Matthew 26:59–68). His statements that he was the Son of God were what the Jews decided was the final proof of Jesus's guilt before the Law: they claimed he blasphemed ("cursed, derided, slandered, and libeled") God by claiming to be the Messiah, the Son of the living God. This they could not deal with. He was everything they believed the Messiah wasn't. And he was nothing they thought the Messiah should be.

Nothing inspired more derision, hatred, and revulsion toward Jesus than his claim to be God incarnate. And nothing brings greater disdain than that claim today. You can call Jesus a good man, a great prophet, a fine leader, perhaps the greatest man who ever lived. But utter the words, "He wasn't just a man, he was God," and you may be in for a fight.

When Jesus asked his disciples, "Who do you say I am?" they answered the expected ways: "a great prophet, Elijah, etc." But Peter said, "You are the Christ, the Son of the living God" (see Matthew 16:13–16). Jesus then told Peter this was the "rock" on which he would build his church. The "rock" wasn't Peter himself but rather the confession of Jesus being the Son of God.

Ultimately, that's the line of demarcation for everyone. "Whom do you say he is?" is the question each of us must answer.

How we answer determines where we will spend eternity.

40

Jesus was one AMAZING preacher.

How would you like to step into church and find out Jesus would be delivering the sermon that day? Do you think he would be compelling? Would he inspire you? Would you come away changed forever?

Well, you can hear Jesus preach. Not audibly, of course, but the Gospels do include ten "discourses" by Jesus. In each he did something a little different, so it's wise to know what subjects he covered. They also give us a taste of what it might have been like to hear him in person.

Matthew 5–7 is the Sermon on the Mount. As his first major sermon recorded, Jesus covered primarily his interpretation of the Law and a number of practical issues like giving, praying, fasting, money, worrying, and the "narrow way." It's a masterpiece of simple wording that's memorable for its many compelling phrases and quotable quotes. When people heard it, they came away amazed, as stated in Matthew 7:28.

Next, in Matthew 10:9–42, we find Jesus talking to his disciples and sending them out into the cities to preach the gospel, heal, cast out demons, and raise the dead. It's a marvel of warnings about what they will face and what it really means to be his disciples.

After that, Matthew 18:2–20 brings together a number of parables and illustrations, a primary focus being: "Unless you change and become like little children, you will never enter the kingdom of heaven" (Matthew 18:3).

Matthew 23:1–39 is Jesus's denouncement of those who rejected him and questioned his ministry—primarily the teachers of the Law and the Pharisees. It's a powerful message that puts these hypocrites firmly in their places, but it was likely meant to move them to repentance and keep others from following their path to destruction.

Matthew 24 and 25 is Jesus's final word to his disciples about the future and how to prepare for his second coming. It includes several parables—the ten virgins, the talents, and the sheep and the goats.

Turning to the book of Luke, we find in chapter 15 a series of three parables—the lost sheep, the lost coin, and the prodigal son. It's a powerful portrait of Jesus's and his Father's feelings about lost people. More parables follow in Luke 16.

Finally we come to the book of John, where we find two messages, including:

- John 5:19–47, where Jesus answered his critics about his authority and his identity, and

- John 13 through 17, called the Upper Room Discourse because he gave it in the upper room where he shared the Last Supper with his disciples. It covers numerous topics, including Jesus's washing the disciples' feet and the nature of servanthood (John 13), where Jesus was going and what it meant to be a disciple (John 14), the vine and the branches and the nature of love (John 15), the work of the Spirit (John 16), and Jesus's final prayer for his disciples (John 17).

Reading Jesus's sermons is like discovering the mother lode. They're witty, quotable, powerful, and compelling. You'll really get to "hear" Jesus, the ultimate preacher.

One of the greatest experiences I've ever had was hearing an actor recite one of Jesus's sermons as if he were Jesus himself. For the first time I gained a real sense of what it must have been like to sit at Jesus's feet.

When you read these messages, think of yourself that way: sitting at Jesus's feet and drinking it all in as if for the first time. Perhaps you'll be as amazed as those listeners some two thousand years ago.

41

Even Jesus NEEDED to pray.

"Dear Father," Jesus prayed. "I'm in a real fix. These disciples are driving me . . . " Did Jesus ever start a prayer like that? Who knows. But considering that Jesus was the second person of the Trinity and in constant touch with his Father, it seems remarkable in a way that he needed to pray. But we have to remember that just as Jesus was fully God, he also was completely human. He felt all the needs, drives, concerns, and temptations of any normal human (yet without ever doing anything wrong).

Thus it shouldn't surprise us that Jesus prayed, probably early every morning. Mark 1:35 refers to one such instance: "Very early in the morning, while it was still dark, Jesus got up, left the house and went off to a solitary place, where he prayed." This was after a long night with crowds that didn't even start arriving until after sunset. Mark says that "the whole town gathered at the door" (Mark 1:33). Jesus healed and drove out demons. Who knows how late he finally got to bed, but Jesus still thought prayer important enough to get up early in the morning, while it was still dark. It seems prayer revitalized and strengthened him physically and spiritually.

That day Jesus started on a preaching tour of Galilee, and he may have known he needed the strength and spiritual power that could only be found in prayer. Maybe he asked God for that strength as he prayed. Or perhaps Jesus discussed with his Father his plan for the day, how his mission was going, what the Father wanted him to do, anything that was on his heart—just like any normal person who has a sense of the importance of prayer.

Later, in Mark 6:45–46, we find that Jesus told his disciples to row across the lake to the other side. Then, "after leaving them, he went up on a mountainside to pray." This happened right after the feeding of the five thousand and shortly before he walked on water. Perhaps that plan was put into Jesus's head by the Spirit during this session—or the spiritual power he needed to walk on water was attained through this time in prayer.

Luke 5:16 makes it clear that such prayer sessions were Jesus's common practice, in contrast with his draining interactions with the crowds: "Jesus often withdrew to lonely places and prayed." Clearly, this was not unusual. In fact, his habit of prayer seemed to so inspire the disciples that they finally requested that he teach them to pray (see Luke 11:1–4). There Luke says, "One day Jesus was praying in a certain place. When he finished, one of his disciples said to him, 'Lord, teach us to pray, just as John taught his disciples.'" And then Luke quotes a prayer that is also quoted in the Sermon on the Mount (see Matthew 6:9–13), which we know as the Lord's Prayer.

Jesus prayed before making important decisions. Before choosing his twelve disciples, Luke 6:12 shows us that Jesus spent the night on a mountainside in prayer. And the Transfiguration happened when Jesus went up on a mountain to pray (see Luke 9:28–36). While Peter, James, and John struggled to stay awake, Jesus prayed with power, and something dramatic happened: "As he was praying, the appearance of his face changed, and his clothes became as bright as a flash of lightning. Two men, Moses and Elijah, appeared in glorious splendor, talking with Jesus. They spoke about his departure, which he was about to bring to fulfillment at Jerusalem" (Luke 9:28–31). Is this symbolic of the kind of communion and personal change that is brought about through prayer?

Finally, Hebrews 5:7 tells us, "During the days of Jesus' life on earth, he offered up prayers and petitions with loud cries and tears to the one who could save him from death, and he was heard because of his reverent submission." God didn't save him from death; he didn't have to, because Jesus reverently submitted to God's will. But we know that God heard him—and helped him, giving him strength, grace, and peace.

Jesus was God, but he still needed to pray. How much more do we?

42

Jesus sometimes got angry— and SHOWED it.

Everyone gets angry. Even Jesus, though he never let it lead him into sin, became angry on several occasions.

The most obvious of these situations were the two times he "cleaned out the temple" (see John 2:13–16 and Luke 19:45–46). The first occurred at the inception of his ministry in Israel and the second happened three years later at the beginning of the week that ended in Jesus's crucifixion. Each time the Bible says he made a whip and drove out the moneychangers and sellers of sacrificial animals.

Exchanging currency and selling animals for temple sacrifices was high finance in those days, and most of it was run by the Sadducees, a Jewish sect that vigorously opposed Jesus. They cheated and stole from godly people who came to make sacrifices in accordance with the laws of Moses. And the Sadducees got the people coming and going. First, they wouldn't accept regular money for purchases; no, you had to use sacred temple money. And guess who controlled that currency—the moneychangers. They didn't even bother to disguise their rotten rate of exchange, because what choice did the people have? Making those temple sacrifices was God's law.

In addition, when people brought their own sacrifice—a dove, a sheep, or a goat—the priests had to inspect the animal to make sure it wasn't blemished, wounded, or handicapped since the law specified that only perfect specimens could be offered. Often these priests found something wrong with the animal and exchanged—for a high price—that animal or bird for one of their "top grade" ones. What they really did was recycle the same animals—one more way to bilk the people.

So when Jesus arrived at the temple and saw this illicit business going on, he was enraged. For a priest, the earthly representative of God, to be a purveyor of stolen goods was not only evil but vicious. So Jesus drove them all out, knocking over their tables and releasing the animals. It made him an instant hero to the people—and an instant enemy to the Jewish leaders.

But Jesus's anger was well directed, and not on his own behalf but on God's. Such anger is sometimes called "righteous indignation," and it's something we all ought to feel when we witness injustice and other evils in our world.

Mark 3:1–6 gives us the only other recorded situation in which Jesus expressed genuine revulsion, disgust, and indignation.

The Pharisees were looking for a reason to harass Jesus, and it seemed they might just have their opportunity. Over time Jewish leaders had cooked up a legion of laws about what was and was not permissible on the Sabbath. (God had commanded that no work be done on that day, but the Pharisees' definition of "work" had grown more and more broad.) On this Sabbath day, Jesus spotted a man with a withered hand sitting near the synagogue, perhaps to beg. He called the man forward and posed this question to the Pharisees: "Which is lawful on the Sabbath: to do good or to do evil, to save a life or to kill?"

The answer should have been obvious, but to people bent on destroying the Son of God, it was the perfect opportunity to catch him in a crime punishable by death (as Sabbath breaking was).

No one said a word.

Jesus "looked around at them in anger and, deeply distressed at their stubborn hearts," he healed the man.

Healing may have been a new item on the Pharisees' Sabbath black list, but it became a bellwether of their hatred for Jesus.

What makes Jesus angry? Using the things of God for selfish gain. Rejecting the work of God to support made-up traditions. Not caring about the plight of hurting people.

And those things should make us angry too.

43

Jesus championed WOMEN'S rights too.

Modern feminists like to think their movement started in the early 1900s and then took off in the 1960s and 70s. However, there's strong evidence that Jesus was a supporter of some feminist ideas, at least in recognizing female equality and value.

We find the first inkling of this in the genealogy of Jesus recorded in Matthew 1:1–16. In the midst of the usual list of male ancestors, Matthew included five women: Tamar, Rahab, Ruth, Bathsheba, and Mary (the mother of Jesus). Though several of these women fail as symbols of purity and perfection (Rahab was a prostitute), it's still remarkable for them to be mentioned at all. Matthew's list shows that a shift in perception had occurred. Why? Because throughout his three-year ministry, Jesus welcomed women of all backgrounds. He treated them as equals, worthy of all the rights and privileges afforded to any male in his kingdom.

We find another suggestion of this shift in John 2:1–10, where Jesus turned water into wine at a wedding in Cana. Here, his mother, Mary, approached him, asking him to solve the problem of the host running out of wine. Normally, in that culture a woman, even a mother, would not have been so forward. But Jesus undoubtedly had long demonstrated an openness to the opinions, thoughts, and feelings of the women around him. His mother felt comfortable asking him to (and had faith that he could) perform a miracle, even when he'd never done one before.

Probably the best example of Jesus's recognition of and respect for women is when he spoke with the Samaritan woman at the well, as recorded in John 4. We aren't told the woman's name, but recording a conversation as lengthy and full as this was unprecedented. Perhaps the most amazing part of the story is the fact that Jesus even spoke to her. This action astonished even the woman herself, for she said to him, "You are a Jew and I am a Samaritan woman. How can you ask me for a drink?" (John 4:9). John slips in the parenthetical aside: "Jews do not associate with Samaritans," but he might just as well have added, "or women." In fact, the average observant Jew of Jesus's day prayed first thing each morning, "Thank you, God, that you did not make me a sinner, a Gentile, or a woman." John 4:27 tells us that even the disciples, who were accustomed to Jesus's unorthodox behavior—were surprised to find Jesus talking with a woman.

The mistreatment women received at the hands of Jewish men is obvious in history as well as in the Gospels. When Jesus healed women on the Sabbath, the outcry from the Law-lovers was immediate and strong. On another occasion a woman was caught in the act of adultery (John 8:1–11) and publicly brought before Jesus (and a crowd) for him to pronounce judgment in accordance with the harsh Mosaic Law—stoning. But notice that no mention is made of the man involved in this adultery. Apparently he had slipped away, probably with the help of the men who apprehended this poor woman to lay a trap for Jesus. Women bore the brunt of the harsher sentences like this one simply because they had less power in the society, were less able to defend themselves physically, and thus were easier to blame.

But Jesus repeatedly healed, helped, and taught women along with men. When Martha asked Jesus to tell her sister, Mary, to stop sitting at Jesus's feet learning—just as male students would do—and start helping her in the kitchen, Jesus reprimanded Martha, not Mary. He told her,

"Mary has chosen what is better, and it will not be taken away from her" (Luke 10:42).

The ultimate result of this outlook came later, as Jesus's followers wrote about him and his teachings. Paul spoke specifically of the equality of women in Galatians 3:28, where he said, "There is neither Jew nor Greek, slave nor free, male nor female, for you are all one in Christ Jesus." That oneness signified respect, equality before God, and a whole new way of looking at women.

44

Jesus's MIRACLES can't be explained away.

Did Jesus's miracles really happen, or were they merely the misperception of ignorant and superstitious minds, as some today would like to believe? Can they all be explained away by educated, rational minds? I remember distinctly my philosophy and religion professor telling our college class that Mary most likely had an affair with a Roman soldier while visiting Jerusalem and then made up the whole "virgin birth" story to cover her tracks. He also told us that many of the miracles happened with people who had "psychosomatic illnesses," or else they were "set up" in much the same way a filmmaker sets up a scene. According to him Jesus was a master plotter. At the time, the book *The Passover Plot* was also available, and he told us to read it. According to this professor, the book offered a reasonable explanation of what really happened on Resurrection Sunday.

I swallowed this hook, line, and sinker for years—until I began to study the record for myself. I went to the original documents as some advised me and just read the New Testament. In it I found some amazing evidence of things I'd never thought about.

The question on my mind for a long time was "Could Jesus truly have set up his miracles? And if so, which ones, and how did he do it?"

For instance, regarding the story of Jesus walking on water the professor told us the preposition *on* in Greek could also be translated "by." So in reality, Jesus was walking "by the water" instead of on it in this so-called miracle.

I went to the passages—the story appears in several gospels—and they all reported the same general conditions: a storm on the sea; disciples rowing madly for shore "in the middle of the lake" (Mark 6:47); during the "fourth watch of the night"—between three and six o'clock in the morning—Jesus came "walking on the lake" (Mark 6:48); the disciples thought it was a ghost; Peter asked to come out to Jesus; Peter lost faith and nearly drowned; Jesus saved him at the last second. I reasoned, How could the disciples have mistaken the "middle of the lake" for "by the shoreline," if that's where Jesus was? Moreover, how did Peter almost drown in a foot of water if he stood by the shore where Jesus was? Finally, why didn't the boat run aground if it was that close to shore? I couldn't see any way this miracle could have been faked.

I began studying the stories of blind men given their sight back, lame men walking, demons coming out of people and shrieking that Jesus was the Son of God and Jesus telling them to be silent, water turned to wine, a storm stilled, and a crowd of five thousand fed. Perhaps it would be possible for someone, under the right conditions, to set up a miracle or two: something easy, like bringing in a man no one knew who said he was blind and then supposedly healing him. But these miracles happened in every imaginable situation—city and country, with men "born blind" and others, like a man lame for thirty-eight years who everyone knew personally, and so on. And there were thousands of them. Some people say Jesus stopped disease and disabilities in Israel for a decade during his three years of healing and compassion.

What really didn't add up to me was the fact that all the writers of these stories—Matthew, Mark, Luke, and John—were persecuted for their faith. Matthew paid for his testimony with his life. We don't know what happened to Mark or Luke, but John was finally banished to a small island in the Mediterranean Sea (Patmos). If these people made up all this stuff, or even exaggerated it—"Well, really, it was this blind guy and he winked a couple of times, but I don't think he ever really saw again.

But we said he did because it made for a more exciting story"—why would they have been willing to pay such a terrible price for their stories in the end? They could simply have said to the authorities, "We made it all up," and they would have been off the hook.

That was the one thing I couldn't get around. If all this material about Jesus was "made up" or "set up" as my professor said, what was the point? People wouldn't have believed such fantastic accounts unless they were actually eyewitnesses to them. And that was the rub. For Matthew, Mark, Luke, and John to go into their studies and produce four versions of the story of Jesus, three of them with many similarities, seems unlikely enough. But if no one else knew about these things, how did word of them get spread around? Who would have taken the stories in hand and made them bestsellers? Why would anyone in his or her right mind have believed them?

I couldn't see it. There were just too many eyewitnesses to these miracles who became the first believers in Christ—three thousand on the Day of Pentecost alone—for it to have been made up or set up. Most of the writings didn't come about until years later anyway. Before that the stories were circulated by word of mouth by those who witnessed the miracles, heard the words, and experienced the person of Jesus. When asked anything about him, everything came spilling out. It wasn't until years later that some writers thought of committing all the material to paper (actually, papyrus or vellum—scraped animal skin). And by then the whole world had already been turned upside down by the story of Jesus as spread by eyewitnesses.

News simply doesn't pass the test of time when people have made it up. It's too easy to debunk. "Find me one guy who saw Jesus alive after he died on the cross!"

"OK, how about five hundred?"

That's what the apostle Paul pointed out when people asked him about Jesus's resurrection. He explained that Jesus "appeared to Peter, and then to the Twelve. After that, he appeared to more than five hundred of the brothers at the same time, most of whom are still living, though some have fallen asleep" (1 Corinthians 15:5–6). In other words, Paul said, "If you don't believe me, consult any of those who actually saw him, because there are plenty of them."

In the final analysis, for Jesus or his disciples to have set up or made up the miracles is in itself an impossible stretch. Too many people saw these things happen—people whose lives were changed—and confirmed them. It would be like someone today writing a book on the life of John F. Kennedy and telling us about all his miracles, great words, death, and resurrection. It simply wouldn't wash because too many people are still alive who knew him and can testify that he didn't do such things.

No, I don't think even Jesus could have pulled off such a set-up. And why would he? It'd be much too complex. For Jesus I'm sure it was easier to do the real miraculous thing.

45

Jesus NEVER made a spectacle of miracles.

Jesus stilled the storm, turned water into wine, and fed five thousand men (to say nothing of women and children) with five pieces of bread and two small bits of fish. He walked on water, cast as many as six thousand demons out of one demon-possessed man, and spit on a blind man to make him see.

But did he ever do anything really flashy?

What do I mean? Something for the cameras. Something to wow the crowd. Something to make a big point and maybe some big bucks.

Never. Every one of Jesus's miracles had practical or physical value: The blind man could see. The lame man could jump and run. The storm stopped and the disciples were saved. The water was turned into wine, saving the wedding host the humiliation of the wine running out. Jesus never did anything for show. In fact, many times he told the people he helped, healed, or delivered not to talk about it to anyone. If anything, Jesus's fame spread by word of mouth in spite of his instructions. Such great crowds came after him to be healed or helped that he often had to flee to the countryside for some refreshment and rest.

All of Jesus's miracles were verifiable by eyewitnesses. Some were performed in a private setting, and Jesus often tried to keep them private (see the story of Jairus's daughter in Mark 5:35–43 and the healing of the blind men in Matthew 9:27–31). But most of his miracles were quite public. The writers of the New Testament even appealed to the public nature of the miracles as a decisive point to prove their veracity (see John 21:24–25; 1 Corinthians 15:3–8; 2 Peter 1:16–21).

All of Jesus's miracles were performed simply, with no fanfare. Yes, there were times when Jesus spit on or put mud on a blind man's eyes, but there must have been some divine reason for those actions, as they were rare. In most instances Jesus waved no wands, drew no bunnies out of top hats. Instead, he merely spoke a word and it happened, the same way God created the world in Genesis 1. God wastes no efforts.

If Jesus had ever wanted to do some "magic" for someone important, he had his chance with King Herod in Luke 23:8–12. Luke tells us Herod was "greatly pleased" when Pilate sent Jesus to him for legal proceedings because "for a long time he had been wanting to see him. From what he had heard about him, he hoped to see him perform some miracle" (Luke 23:8). Jesus could have made a giant hand appear in the air (like God did with King Belshazzar—see Daniel 5:1–31) and slap that man silly. But he didn't. He just stood there saying nothing, enduring the mockery and taunts while refusing to do anything that smacked of sensationalism.

What did he do? Jesus's miracles were all unique. Different people, different circumstances, different diseases. He made each miracle an event without turning it into a sensation. He touched the lepers, who'd had to cry out, "Unclean, unclean!" wherever they went and had not felt a human's gentle touch and care for years. He conversed with the blind and the lame, often asking them precisely what they wanted—and did they believe? He dealt with crowds and individuals, soldiers and tax collectors. He turned no one away. He even walked up to people and offered to heal them without their asking for it or knowing who he was.

Jesus's miracles were personal. He didn't wave his hand over a crowd and say, "Be gone, demons, blindness, lameness; and if other need is represented here, take care of that too," like some modern healing evangelists do. No, he dealt with each person individually. He asked questions. He touched them. He listened to them. That's why he was tired so much of the time. Although Jesus could have walked into town, held up his hand, closed his eyes, and intoned, "God, heal them all," he didn't do it that way. His mission went far beyond just healing bodies; he came to heal souls, and that took a personal touch.

Think about it. Jesus could have become the greatest magician/ miracle worker/Houdini of all time. He had the power to perform any trick the crowd wanted. And they would have kept him busy throughout all eternity.

But Jesus didn't come to entertain the world. He came to save it. And thus his miracles did nothing less than point the way to that salvation.

46

Sometimes Jesus's disciples DISAPPOINTED him.

Jesus's disciples witnessed miracles of power, heard words of incredible wisdom, and experienced a love of giant proportions; yet they still doubted, still questioned, still wondered. They were people just like us—skeptical, fearful, unsure.

When Jesus ordered his disciples to cross the Sea of Galilee in a fishing boat, they knew precisely what to do. They were fishermen. They had done this a million times. They pulled out the oars and began rowing for all they were worth.

Jesus, perhaps exhausted from teaching and healing all day, fell asleep in the stern of the boat. I imagine the rowers even working to keep the oars from squeaking too loudly, so as not to wake him. They knew what he'd been through—jostling crowds, insistent followers, hopeful but prodding supplicants, and shrewd and rumor-spreading critics. The disciples decided to let Jesus sleep till the cows came home or the boat reached shore, whichever came first.

But then something unexpected happened. A vicious storm whipped the waters into a cauldron of foam and fury (see Matthew 8:23–27). The Sea of Galilee, because of the steep mountains that surround it, often is lashed with sudden and powerful storms. The valleys in the mountains act as funnels for the wind, and the sea churns up quickly.

As the men oared with all their strength for land, menacing waves engulfed the boat. Water sloshed over the sides, and the fishermen bailed furiously. But the storm was too much for them. Picture the scene:

"We're going to sink!"

"We've got to do something."

"But what?"

Suddenly every eye fixed on Jesus, sleeping soundly (if wetly) in the back of the boat. How could he not have awoken? Could he be that tired?

"Should we wake him up?" one shouted over the howling wind.

"Maybe he can do something," another said.

"Like what?" others wanted to know.

"Maybe he can get us to land quickly," the first answered. "Or stop the boat from sinking."

"Yeah, right," one of the less confident disciples answered. "He'll probably just be irritated we woke him up."

One of them finally corked up the courage to shake Jesus awake and ask for help. Can you see this disciple stumbling through the quickly filling boat to give Jesus a gentle tap? "Uh . . . Lord?"

Jesus just snoozed on.

"Master!" A little shove this time.

"*Jesus, we're going to sink!*" This time the guy fell into Jesus's lap as the boat lurched from the slap of an angry wave.

Jesus woke up, glanced around at things, quickly sized up the situation, then stood and commanded the wind: "Quiet! Be still."

Do you think it was a sigh, a whisper, or a bellow? We don't know. But immediately the wind died down, the waves stopped frothing, and the sea became smooth as glass.

Then Jesus said, "Why are you so afraid? Do you still have no faith?"

The disciples probably paled, or maybe blushed—but among themselves they must have gaped with astonishment, whispering to each other and wondering what sort of man this was who could stop a storm.

Who wouldn't be amazed?

But do you know what I think is the most astonishing part? How long they waited to arouse Jesus. When Jesus asked them why they had so little faith, I wonder if he didn't mean their fear of the storm but rather their being afraid to wake him and get him involved. Did they think he'd be angry, or that he'd chew them out for waking him out of happy dreams when they should have simply bailed harder?

What was Jesus's point? Perhaps: why didn't you wake me sooner, when the problem didn't require a major miracle?

How often, for many of us, prayer is the last resort. We don't kneel before the throne of grace until our situation requires miraculous intervention. What we don't realize is that God wants us to come to him first, not last.

What encouragement there is in the approachable God of the Bible! He never chastises us for coming to him about a problem. He never shouts that he doesn't have the time or snaps, "Whaddaya want this time?" No, God is utterly and always accessible, whenever we need his help.

I find that amazing. Why would the God of the universe ever concern himself with my problems, my needs? And yet that is the essence of the gospel, isn't it? The God of all creation cares about you and me. No, more than that. He loves us so completely that he sent Jesus to pay the ultimate price to obtain our friendship and faith in him. Nothing—absolutely nothing—is too small for his attention, and nothing—absolutely nothing—is too big and complicated for him to take on.

Why is God like this? Because he was one of us too. Jesus knows what it's like to be human. He understands our fears and our worries. And he wants us to know that his understanding leads not to contempt but to compassion. Even when we wait too long, he remains ready to take action.

47

Jesus RESCUED a lame man at a pool.

One would think the first requirement for being healed would be to go to God and ask for it. But with Jesus that was not always the case.

In John 5:1–15 we find the story of an invalid by the pool of Bethesda (meaning "house of outpouring") as a case in point. The pool was near the Sheep Gate of Jerusalem, located in the north wall of the city. At that pool a multitude of disabled people rested, lolled, and lounged, waiting for the pool to ripple. When the water stirred, people believed an angel had arrived, and the first person to slide into the pool would be healed. Some scholars today believe this pool was fed by a spring, which explains the stirring effect. The water was also red in color, which some believed indicated a medicinal quality.

The man in question had been an invalid for thirty-eight years. When Jesus saw him and learned how long he had suffered in that condition, he simply walked up to the man and asked him, "Do you want to get well?" (John 5:6).

"Sir," the invalid replied, "I have no one to help me into the pool when the water is stirred. While I am trying to get in, someone else goes down ahead of me" (John 5:7). Perhaps the man hoped Jesus would stick around and help him get into the water on the outside chance that he'd be first and be healed. It seems he had no clue who Jesus was or how close he was to true healing power.

Jesus didn't wait another moment, and he didn't wait for the troubling of the waters. He simply said, "Get up! Pick up your mat, and walk" (John 5:8).

And that was it. The man was cured instantly. He obeyed, picked up his mat, and began walking about. Some critics saw this, however, and since this healing took place on a Sabbath, they complained: "It is the Sabbath; the law forbids you to carry your mat" (John 5:10).

The former invalid replied, "The man who made me well said to me, 'Pick up your mat and walk'" (John 5:11).

Of course they wanted to know who the fellow was who had done this (as if there were lots of guys running around healing people who had been invalids for years). But the man didn't know who Jesus was, and Jesus had slipped away into the crowd. Later Jesus reappeared and, finding the man, told him, "See, you are well again. Stop sinning or something worse may happen to you" (John 5:14). Then the man went and told the Jews that the person who had healed him was Jesus.

Note a couple of elements here. First, unlike the blind man from John 9, this man's affliction had apparently been caused by sin. Jesus knew about it, presumably because of his divine omniscience. He sternly warned the man not to sin again.

Second, it's interesting that each time the Jews persecuted someone Jesus had healed on the Sabbath, Jesus located the person later and gave him some encouragement or warning (see also John 9:35–41). Jesus, the ultimate Shepherd, didn't leave his sheep on their own to fend for themselves; he came to their rescue in the end. That's a principle found throughout Scripture. Jesus simply will not allow one of his own to be snatched out of his hands.

48

Jesus healed even when he WASN'T trying.

Did you know Jesus was so powerful that he once healed a woman when he wasn't even trying—didn't even really know she was there?

He was busy with someone else, an important person in the town who needed help desperately. As usual, great crowds were pressing in on Jesus, wanting to see him work miracles, wanting to hear him speak. But one anonymous woman was there on a special, secret mission.

It occurred one day as Jesus walked through town and a synagogue official came to him, asking him to help his daughter, who was gravely ill. Jesus and the man took off in the direction of the man's home. But as they were hurrying on their way, something unexpected happened.

A woman who had been "subject to bleeding for twelve years" (Mark 5:25) came up behind Jesus. Hers was probably some kind of irregular vaginal bleeding, which was even more than embarrassing in those days than it might be today, because when a woman had her period, she was considered "unclean." Anyone who touched her would also be made unclean, so the woman's illness sentenced her to a life of isolation and misery. It's possible such an ailment could have kept this woman from marrying and having children. She undoubtedly was an outcast, and to her life of indignity was added poverty. She had spent everything she had trying to cure this problem. Mark 5:26 says, "She had suffered a great deal under the care of many doctors, and had spent all she had, yet instead of getting better she grew worse."

This highly emotional kind of affliction led the woman to seek out Jesus, but in a special way. She didn't want to draw attention to herself. Perhaps she was afraid Jesus wouldn't touch and heal her if he knew of her unclean condition. Even if she thought Jesus might show compassion to her, any contact with a crowd would be a risky proposition. If they found out they were rubbing shoulders with an unclean woman, surely some would be upset—maybe becoming insulting or even growing violent. She didn't want to be at the center of any public spectacle. And she certainly didn't want everyone knowing what she had come for in the first place.

So, while the crowd pressed in around Jesus, this woman managed to sneak in and touch the fringe of his cloak. Why? Because, she said to herself, "If I just touch his clothes, I will be healed" (Mark 5:28).

Can you comprehend what tremendous faith this woman had? She believed so much in Jesus's power to heal that she risked much public censure to try for something that had never happened before—by merely touching Jesus's clothing, she knew she could be healed. Where might she have gotten such an idea?

Devout Jews wore tassels on the four corners of their robes to remind them to obey God's commandments (see Numbers 15:38–40; Deuteronomy 22:12). So this woman might have believed there was some special, sacred power in them when worn by a person like Jesus. Or perhaps she was trying to reach out to Jesus without actually touching him and making him unclean by her condition.

After touching his robe, the woman knew that her bleeding had stopped and that she was finally free from her suffering. But that wasn't the end of the story. Her undercover, quiet quest for healing was about to be exposed, her cover blown, her anonymity ended.

Jesus turned around.

"Who touched my clothes?"

He had realized at once that healing power had gone out from him. But his question astonished the crowd, because multitudes were touching him, pressing against him, reaching out to him. Maybe others believed some blessing would come from his touch, as Jesus often healed by merely touching someone with his hand. But Jesus kept looking around to see who had touched him through faith for healing.

The woman knew this was all about her. Would he be angry? Would he condemn her? But she had been healed—undeniably, miraculously, wonderfully healed. So she fell at Jesus's feet and confessed that she had been the one to touch him and that his power had healed her of her infirmity—just the sort of publicity she, as an outcast, had tried so hard to avoid.

But Jesus didn't chide her. Instead, he reassured her and praised her faith. He said, "Daughter, your faith has healed you. Go in peace and be freed from your suffering" (Mark 5:34).

She stepped back into the crowd, Jesus continued on his way, and no more was said about it. The problem that had consumed her life, that had laid her low and consigned her to the fringe of society for twelve long years was a simple matter for Jesus to handle. He healed her without even trying.

That's a good thing to remember when our problems seem to big for us to handle.

49

Jesus had a soft spot in his heart for CHILDREN.

How does Jesus feel about kids? We can find the answer in his own words: "Let the little children come to me" (Matthew 19:14). "Whoever humbles himself like this child is the greatest in the kingdom of heaven" (Matthew 18:4). "Whoever welcomes one of these little children in my name welcomes me" (Mark 9:37). "I tell you the truth, unless you change and become like little children, you will never enter the kingdom of heaven" (Matthew 18:3). But I think the story recorded in Mark 5 is the best illustration of how Jesus felt about children.

On this occasion Jesus raised a little girl from the dead. When the twelve-year-old daughter of Jairus, a synagogue ruler and all-around VIP, was stricken with a deadly illness, the leader's thoughts turned to the one person on earth who could help her: Jesus. He sought out Jesus, fell at his feet, and implored him earnestly to come and heal the girl. Undoubtedly touched by this father's plight and his love for his daughter, Jesus immediately set out with Jairus for his house.

After a slight delay in which Jesus healed a woman, some men came from Jairus's house with bad news: "Your daughter is dead. . . . Why bother the teacher any more?" (Mark 5:35). Jesus ignored what they said and reassured Jairus, "Don't be afraid, just believe" (Mark 5:36).

They continued on to Jairus's home, where people had gathered to mourn the little girl's death. They wailed loudly, in the Jewish tradition. But Jesus didn't join in their mourning. Instead, he said to them, "Why all this commotion and wailing? The child is not dead but asleep" (Mark 5:39).

The sounds of mourning turned to laughter at Jesus's impossible statement. Asleep? Didn't Jesus think they could tell when someone was really, truly, stone-cold dead? The word used here for "laughing" means "laughed him to scorn" or "ridiculed him." This was a complete reversal—from mourning to raucous laughter. Isn't it amazing how quickly a crowd can change? Part of that was because in those days the Jews hired people (much like Muslims do today) to function as official mourners. They had little concern for the deceased or the family but were paid to put on plenty of weeping to show how loved the person was who had died.

Jesus would have none of it. He put the people out and took only the parents and three disciples (Peter, James, and John) inside. He took the young girl by the hand and said to her, "Talitha koum!" (which means, "Little girl, I say to you, get up!") (Mark 5:41).

Without so much as a sigh, the little girl stood up and walked around, according to the version in Mark. (This story is also recorded in Matthew 9:18–26 and Luke 8:40–56). As you can imagine, her parents were astonished. Jesus "gave strict orders not to let anyone know about this, and told them to give her something to eat" (Mark 5:43).

"Give her something to eat." Apparently, death makes people hungry! But beyond that, look at the simple beauty of this statement. In all the commotion—the parents' shock and joy, their embracing the girl and holding her close, as if to never let her go again; perhaps the disciples were astonished into immobility, or maybe they were chattering excitedly among themselves—the girl herself is almost forgotten in the shadow of this stupendous, incredible miracle. But Jesus hadn't forgotten: he knew just what she needed. She had been sick for many days; she had been ravaged by illness and weakened by not eating. Perhaps before her death, her body had used up all the nourishment she'd taken in. Now that she was totally restored, Jesus was keenly aware of what the little girl needed and wanted: she was hungry!

I find Jesus's personal touch amazing and exciting. Not only was he concerned with the child's health and well-being, he was also concerned with her comfort. While everyone else jumped around and screamed with glee, he stood at the center of the hurrahs with practical things on his mind. He knows the hearts and needs of everyone, but perhaps especially children, who are more helpless than adults to meet their own needs. Jesus seems to have had a soft spot in his heart for the kids around him. He understood their interests and needs and met them.

I sometimes wonder how things will play out when each of us gets to heaven, raised from the dead to be there. What will Jesus have waiting for us? I think it'll be the perfect first gift of heaven. We'll wake up to something like Christmas Day, and Christ will be standing there, grinning and enjoying his beloved children's joy.

50

Jesus was accused of being the DEVIL himself.

Think of what it must have been like to be living in Israel at the time of Jesus's ministry. If you had anything wrong with you—blindness, deafness, lameness, demon-possession, bad skin, a constant cold, chronic bleeding, whatever—and you heard about Jesus, you set aside whatever reservations you might have had and went to see him. The Bible tells us of Jesus's mission of mercy to the sick and suffering: "Laying his hands on each one, he healed them" (Luke 4:40).

Even if you happened to be healthy, listening to Jesus speak must have been a marvelous experience. Mark 10:24 tells us that the disciples were "amazed at Jesus's words." It's easy to understand why the things Jesus said would amaze those who heard them. He spoke as one who had authority (Mark 1:27) and turned the petty traditions of the Pharisees and Sadducees upside down. He gave the despondent hope, the loser another chance, the sinner redemption, and the lost a direct line to God. Even today the words of Jesus—the ones printed in red in many Bibles—ring with truth, joy, fulfillment, love, compassion, spiritual power, and a clear sense of who God is and what he wants from us. Crowds gathered just to hear Jesus speak.

In some cases multitudes witnessed mighty miracles that displayed Jesus's power over nature—feeding crowds of four thousand (Matthew 15:29–39) and five thousand (Matthew 14:13–21), calming the sea (Mark 4:35–41), walking on water (Matthew 14:22–27), and raising the dead (Mark 5:35–43; Luke 7:11–17; John 11:38–44). At no other time in history did God display his power so frequently. In the three years Jesus ministered in Israel, he never turned away anyone. And we know that he performed many more miracles than just those recorded in the New Testament.

Now suppose you've gone to the lectures. You've seen several actual miracles, right before your eyes. You've met Jesus, heard him argue with some of your friends; perhaps you've even sat and dined with him. How is it possible that you could come to the conclusion that Jesus was the devil in disguise?

Yet this is precisely what some of the leaders in Jesus's day accused him of being. Early in Jesus's ministry various scribes said, "He is possessed by Beelzebub," and "By the prince of demons he is driving out demons"(Mark 3:22).

How could they try to explain Jesus away like this?

If you look closely, you'll find that each time the leaders spoke of Jesus being the devil or being possessed by the devil, Jesus had just said or done something that exposed them for the frauds they were. For instance, in Mark 3:1–19 we read that Jesus healed on the Sabbath, cast out demons, and called and commissioned twelve disciples, giving them power to do miracles of all sorts. Jesus chose humble, common, uneducated men to do God's work—completely passing over the scribes, Pharisees, and Sadducees, the religious leaders who were supposed to be working for God. Not one of them was invited into Jesus's inner circle. Perhaps the leaders felt slighted. How could Jesus choose a bunch of roughneck fishermen over educated, religious people like themselves? How could Jesus give this awesome power to a hated tax collector like Matthew and not give even a smidgen of the same power to one of them?

At other times Jesus infuriated the leaders of the Jews by messing with their business. His clearing the temple of moneychangers and merchants was a direct assault on the means and work of many of the top leaders. Jesus repeatedly confronted the Pharisees about the picky man-made rules they rigidly followed and enforced, and he never condemned his own disciples for breaking those rules. Jesus meddled with their stuff, and that raised their ire.

OK, but to say he was a devil, the son of a devil, possessed by a devil, when all he did was good?

The problem is, Jesus did most of his good for broken, hurting, fringe people. He rarely did it for Pharisees, more because of their opposition and antagonism than because he wouldn't or couldn't. He also didn't invite them into his inner circle. Instead, he slammed them as hypocrites at every turn, and in public places.

Still, saying Jesus was demon-possessed seems shocking and mean. Who could believe it?

Some people did, namely the people who mattered in that culture: the rich, the powerful, the famous. Many of them had few needs and therefore little need of Jesus. And to have someone as famous and powerful as Jesus call them hypocrites—right in front of all those losers—could not be tolerated.

They had to do something about it. Jesus got his power from somewhere, and if they admitted it was from God, they had no good reason to resist or reject Jesus. But he'd insulted them. He'd revealed them to be small-minded, self-serving bad guys, and that just wouldn't do.

So they turned on him. They claimed he was the real bad guy.

The religious leaders constantly tried to undermine Jesus's ministry. Fortunately, God can't be stopped by mere men, however rich or powerful they are. The great teacher of the Pharisees (and even of the apostle Paul), when confronted with the original Jesus movement as it spread throughout his world, said in Acts 5:38–39, "Leave these men alone! Let them go! For if their purpose or activity is of human origin, it will fail. But if it is from God, you will not be able to stop these men; you will only find yourselves fighting against God."

In a similar way, we can fight against God when we despise or put down other ministries we may not agree with just because they're different or see certain parts of Christian doctrine a little differently than we do. Sometimes it's best to keep our mouths shut about others and give ourselves to the work God has given to us. If the Pharisees and Sadducees had done that, they might have found themselves more focused on heaven and less mired in controversy of their own making.

51

Jesus's FAMILY thought he was nuts.

Mary was a Jewish mother. And what is a Jewish mother most proud of? Her firstborn son, of course. He's the one she compares everyone in the family to. "Now, Joseph, you need to follow Jesus's example. Why just the other day . . . " "If you kids were like Jesus, you would never say such things!" And so on.

Ah, Jesus was a dream kid. He always did everything right. He was sinless, and he never sinned against anyone in his family. So they surely held him in the highest esteem, correct?

Well, not exactly. Undoubtedly, the usual jealousies occurred in that family. "Oh, Jesus is just perfect! That's what you think, Mom, isn't it?" And, "If I hear of one more good deed Jesus did, I'm going to spit nails!" And, "It's Jesus this and Jesus that. If I hear his name one more time . . . "

Yes, and then there's the utter uniqueness of Jesus. Surely Mary and Joseph must have told the rest of the family about the remarkable way in which Jesus came to be born. Even if they didn't give too many details, perhaps they scolded the kids about calling Jesus names or complaining about him with words like "If you only knew who he is, you wouldn't say such things." "Well, who is he?" "It's too complicated—I'll explain it when you're older."

Finally there was what happened when Jesus went off to do his own ministry. He healed the sick. He raised the dead. He spoke in a way no one had ever heard before. Crowds followed him. People called him the "son of David," and "the Messiah," and "the Son of the living God."

Unfortunately, those family members knew Jesus long before he ever became famous. They'd been around him from day one. And even if he was sinless and unique, he still didn't seem like rabbi material. He wasn't a priest. He had hardly any education. What did he think he was doing, going around rabble-rousing and performing these amazing feats and miracles no one could explain?

Maybe that's where it started. After calling and commissioning his twelve disciples, Jesus came down from a mountain and entered into a house with his disciples. But lo and behold, such a crowd formed that Jesus and his disciples were not even able to eat (Mark 3:20). "When his family heard about this, they went to take charge of him, for they said, 'He is out of his mind'" (Mark 3:21).

Or in less kind terms, "He's a lunatic. Someone throw him in the looney bin and throw away the key!"

And why did they think this? Because crowds followed him, he healed them all, and he preached. So many people turned out—the seekers, the wannabes, the disciples, the complainers, the critics, the skeptics, all of them—that Jesus's own family thought he had to be crazy to hang out with these nuts. After all, probably plenty of the people who followed Jesus were "fringe" kind of people. Why didn't Jesus conduct a respectable ministry, go to school, become a rabbi, and teach in a synagogue? That was more like what they wanted, even expected.

But Jesus went out there, waded into the throng of needy people, and began fixing everyone and everything in sight. How was it possible? After all, who but the mighty Moses and Elijah and Elisha had actually done miracles? And they had done miracles on a big scale—parting the Red Sea, the destruction of four hundred prophets of Baal, and the blinding of the Syrian army—not this personal stuff where he touched lepers and made them well, transformed down-and-outers and hangers-on, made the lame leap, etc. These people that crammed the synagogue to listen to him were out for nobody but themselves. This couldn't be God's work;

it had to be some kind of trick Jesus had learned on the road, or maybe even—perish the thought—what the Pharisees themselves said: "He is possessed by Beelzebub! By the prince of demons he is driving out demons" (Mark 3:22).

Well, what do you do when your family or other loved ones misunderstand, misjudge, and sell you short?

You do what Jesus did: you live with it. You give them their say, and then you go and do what God has called you to. That's how Jesus handled it.

Sometime later Jesus's family came around. James (author of the book of James) and Jude (author of the book of Jude) were both brothers of Jesus, born to Mary and Joseph. Mary loyally stuck with Jesus to the end, even watching from the foot of the cross as he died his agonizing death. After the initial shock and coming to grips with the reality of Jesus's incredible ministry, perhaps his family went back home and thought about it. Eventually they realized this couldn't be the work of a lunatic, or even a liar. He had to be the real thing: Lord.

52

Jesus warned of an "UNFORGIVABLE" sin.

When some of the leading Jews said Jesus cast out demons by the prince of demons, Beelzebub, and that Jesus was possessed by a demon, the Lord gave them a stern warning about ascribing the works of God to Satan: "I tell you the truth, all the sins and blasphemies of men will be forgiven them. But whoever blasphemes against the Holy Spirit will never be forgiven; he is guilty of an eternal sin" (Mark 3:28–29).

Even today some Christians think they've committed "the unpardonable sin" because of something they did—adultery, theft, lying, whatever. They believe this especially intensely if they had a "besetting sin," one they committed over and over again—lying, sexual sin, stealing, drunkenness, or addiction.

Is it possible to commit blasphemy against the Holy Spirit today, and what exactly was Jesus talking about?

Blaspheming the Holy Spirit is attributing to the devil something the Spirit has done. For instance, if you saw a miracle the Spirit had performed and immediately concluded, "This is the work of the devil," that's blasphemy.

But it goes deeper than that. What exactly had these Jews done?

First, they had seen Jesus work miracles, many of which were healing blind, lame, deaf, and mute people. These were all good, decent, and compassionate acts by Jesus. Yet some of the Pharisees said that since Jesus did them on a Sabbath (the "day of rest"—Saturday in the Jewish week), he must be from the devil, because no righteous person would violate the Sabbath.

These people knew such works could only be from God. For instance, in John 11:47–48 we find the Jews conspiring together against Jesus: "What are we accomplishing?" they asked. "Here is this man performing many miraculous signs. If we let him go on like this, everyone will believe in him, and then the Romans will come and take away both our place and our nation." Clearly, they understood Jesus's "signs" to be genuine miracles that were leading thousands of people to put their faith in him. However, their only concern was whether they would lose their privileged positions of leadership, a purely self-centered and shortsighted motive.

The Jewish leaders saw Jesus drive demons out of many demon-possessed people. Often these demons, in wrenching free of a human, shrieked out that Jesus was the Son of God. Considering that these influential Jews were constantly scrutinizing Jesus, they must have heard this. But they came to the wrong conclusion: "He is possessed by Beelzebub! By the prince of demons he is driving out demons" (Mark 3:22).

Once again, despite seeing miracles and hearing that the demons knew Jesus was the Son of God, these Jews still pronounced him to be of the devil. Perhaps it was a case of believing what you want to believe. Fear of losing their position and nation led them to grasp at straws that led them to oppose Jesus. Or maybe they didn't really believe it themselves but were trying to turn the less educated crowds against Jesus. If the religious leaders said these miracles were the work of Satan, not God, maybe some people would believe them and forsake Jesus.

These leaders had been privileged to hear Jesus's words in person. They'd heard him preach such great sermons as the Sermon on the Mount (see Matthew 5–7). Even common people could tell that Jesus was the real deal. "The crowds were amazed at his teaching, because he taught as one who had authority, and not as their teachers of the Law" (Matthew

7:28–29). In spite of this—or maybe partly because of it—the leaders still said Jesus was led and empowered by the devil.

In the end the Jewish leaders also knew about Jesus's death on the cross and his miraculous resurrection. But when confronted with this, they bribed the soldiers who had guarded Jesus's tomb but were powerless to keep him from rising from the dead. "You are to say, 'His disciples came during the night and stole him away while we were asleep.' If this report gets to the governor, we will satisfy him and keep you out of trouble" (Matthew 28:13–14). So the soldiers did as they were told: they took the money and spread the story the chief priests had concocted to discredit Jesus yet again—even though they knew the truth. And the story they created was "widely circulated among the Jews to this very day" (Matthew 28:15).

These men had seen all sorts of miracles, knew that the only possible explanation was that they were from God, heard the demons and saw them come out of people, and even listened to Jesus's powerful words. But they came to the conclusion that it was all of Satan.

Why was this an unforgivable sin? Because the only way to obtain forgiveness from God is to believe in Jesus, his death for our sins, and his resurrection from the dead. If you believe Jesus is a devil and all his work to be inspired by Satan, you can't possibly believe in him as the Savior of the world. Therefore, you have cut yourself off from the only way to be forgiven.

Can people commit this sin today? I believe they can. If a person studies the New Testament, reads the main stories, digests the truth about Jesus, gets everything down and really understands what and who Jesus was and then says, "He was a devil," it's the same offense.

53

Jesus doesn't fault a guy who DOUBTS.

You'd think that John the Baptist of all people (and prophets) would have known unequivocally that Jesus was the one who would save the world. John had been there when Jesus was baptized and had seen heaven opened and heard the voice of God from heaven announcing, "This is my Son, whom I love; with him I am well pleased" (Matthew 3:17). And John repeatedly told others that Jesus was the expected one, the Messiah, the King of kings and Lord of lords.

John was solid. If you wanted the straight stuff, the real deal, you went to John. He never equivocated, never doubted, never split hairs. For him, Jesus was the Man.

We see that pretty clearly until we happen on Luke 7:18–23, where John, languishing in prison for speaking the truth boldly to King Herod, sent several of his disciples to Jesus to ask a surprising question: "Are you the one who was to come, or should we expect someone else?" (Luke 7:19).

How could this be? Was John really doubting that Jesus was the Messiah? After all he had seen, heard, and preached? Of all people, John was a rock of faith and strength.

Or was he?

Think about the situation. John had welcomed the ministry of Jesus with open arms. He did everything he could to steer his own disciples toward Jesus. He knew that his role was to fade away while Jesus became the center of all things (see John 3:30). John accepted all that despite the fact that he'd had a successful ministry that drew large crowds from every corner of Israel. He'd baptized hundreds, perhaps thousands, as the head of the first prophetic ministry in Israel in more than four hundred years. He'd made a big splash, and the Jewish world buzzed with the news about him—all he said, all he did.

But now he was in prison. He'd run afoul of Herod Antipas, the governor of Judea, by confronting the man about his immoral marriage to his brother's wife, Herodias. Herod's wife was incensed. How dare this man say her marriage was not lawful (see Mark 6:18). "Herodias nursed a grudge against John and wanted to kill him. But she was not able to" (Mark 6:19). Why not? "Because Herod feared John and protected him, knowing him to be a righteous and holy man. When Herod heard John, he was greatly puzzled; yet he liked to listen to him" (Mark 6:20). Apparently Herod didn't much mind the hot words John flung at him.

We don't know how long John suffered there in prison with nothing but time to ponder his situation and his options, but it seems John became discouraged. Perhaps his gloomy, depressing surroundings, his isolation and feelings of helplessness, and his inability to understand how this could be part of God's plan for his life and ministry contributed to John's discouragement and possibly even depression. If you've ever been in a disappointing, difficult, unfathomable place, you can probably empathize with John. When you feel that way, you often sense a great distance between you and God. He no longer seems present, speaking to you, encouraging you. That distance makes the depression even deeper and your own hang-ups, worries, and fears multiply. I know, because something like that happened to me for two and a half years when I attended seminary. When I prayed, there was no responding voice in my heart, assuring me, comforting me. My mind felt afire with every negative thought it could muster, and I suffered in a maelstrom of my own imagined terrors and anxieties.

I wonder if that was what John felt in his own heart.

If it was, it's no small wonder that suddenly he started to question whether Jesus could really be the Messiah. After all, didn't the Messiah come to set the captives free? And who was the most notable, unfairly imprisoned captive in the land? Why, it was John the Baptist himself. If Jesus really was the Messiah, why hadn't Jesus done something to free John?

Perhaps it all spiraled down into a morass of self-pity and anguish. John may have felt lost on a roiling sea of darkness and doom. He knew Jesus was more important than him. He had truly believed that Jesus was the Messiah. But John had faithfully fulfilled his part of the bargain. When was God going to fulfill his? Had John been wrong? This was not at all what he had expected.

So John asked his question through several loyal disciples. And Jesus, in the middle of healing, preaching, and setting the country ablaze with his message, told them, "Go back and report to John what you have seen and heard: The blind receive sight, the lame walk, those who have leprosy are cured, the deaf hear, the dead are raised, and the good news is preached to the poor. Blessed is the man who does not fall away on account of me" (Luke 7:22–23).

Jesus didn't put the man down for his doubts and fears. Instead, he gave John some hard facts—facts that fulfilled the prophecies of Isaiah 35:5–6 and 61:1 regarding what to expect when the Messiah came. John himself may have seen some of Jesus's miracles; at the very least, he'd heard about them. Eyewitnesses reported back to him about Jesus's ministry all the time. So Jesus answered John's doubts about the Messiah with facts he could see and hear about. And then Jesus gave him a great word of encouragement and challenge: "Blessed is the man who does not fall away on account of me" (Luke 7:23). What does that mean?

Go back to those four little words: "on account of me." That's the thrust of the whole statement. One of the great reasons people didn't follow Jesus then, and don't to this day, is that he doesn't meet their expectations. The Jews of Jesus's day expected a political Messiah who would vanquish Rome and set the Hebrew nation free. Instead, they got a caring and compassionate Messiah who ministered to the poor and preached a religion of repentance, faith, and servanthood. For some, this didn't add up to what they thought the Messiah would do or be. So they rejected him.

John had his own expectations, some of which were right on. What John didn't expect was being put on the sidelines permanently in prison. The loneliness and solitude, the deplorable prison conditions, and the loss of hope all likely worked together to make him rethink and question what he had believed earlier.

When we feel miserable and abandoned and some of our cherished beliefs have disappointed us, it can be difficult to distinguish between those things that we were wrong about and those that are unshakably, eternally true.

Fortunately, Jesus could help John. And that's precisely what he did. I'm sure John died a man full of faith and expectation of reigning with Christ in the kingdom of heaven.

But what about you? Have your expectations about Jesus led you to push him into a corner? Have you been praying or thinking things that haven't borne out, and for that reason you're depressed and discouraged?

Keep these words in your heart: "Blessed is the man who does not fall away on account of me." *Blessed* is a word that means "happy, fortunate." In today's vernacular, we might say you're blessed because God intends to send good things your way, the things he most wants to send you. Those things might not be what you prayed for or what you hoped for. But like John, you'll find that they nourish and build you up so that you can withstand the dark night you may be going through.

54

Jesus is ASTONISHED by genuine faith.

Can anything amaze the God of the universe?

Yes, one thing.

We find it in a story about a centurion who asked Jesus to heal one of the man's servants (Matthew 8:5–13). We don't know the servant's specific ailment, but he lay suffering and paralyzed at home. The centurion, a Roman commander of one hundred soldiers, had somehow heard of Jesus the miracle worker, and he didn't hesitate to run to him for help.

The account in Luke 7:1–10 tells us that initially several Jewish friends of the centurion sought out Jesus and found him, pressing him to come and heal the servant. They added sincerely that this centurion had come to the aid of the Jewish people and "deserved" this favor—as if a person's worthiness would command Jesus's help. In fact, throughout the New Testament, we find Jesus healing and helping people from all walks of life. He never favored anyone because they were worthy or righteous.

Jesus headed toward to the centurion's home when more people arrived from the commander, this time to tell him, "Lord, I do not deserve to have you come under my roof. But just say the word, and my servant will be healed. For I myself am a man under authority, with soldiers under me. I tell this one, 'Go,' and he goes; and that one, 'Come,' and he comes. I say to my servant, 'Do this,' and he does it."

When Jesus heard this statement, the text says, "he was astonished." The word *astonished* literally means, "struck dumb with amazement." Jesus was astounded at this man's expression of faith and trust.

Now wait a minute. Wasn't Jesus God incarnate? Didn't he know all about this centurion before the man ever came to him? Wasn't Jesus all-knowing?

Aside from theological arguments about how much of Jesus's divinity was active at any given moment, the simple truth is that Jesus was awed by the centurion's faith. How can that be? How can God be amazed at anything that happens in his world? Isn't amazement and surprise and all that a bit ungodlike? I mean, after all, Jesus knows the end from the beginning and has literally seen it all. Should something as simple as this astonish him?

Yes, and why not? Consider this centurion a moment longer. His faith belongs in the Hall of Fame. He believed Jesus could heal his servant without even being on the spot—something no one had yet seen. Moreover, he came to Jesus with confidence: he not only believed Jesus *could* heal but that he *would* heal, perhaps a minor difference in word usage, but a large one in reality. This guy possessed the real item. He believed on a level that even Jesus hadn't seen in all of Israel.

Why is faith such a biggie in God's eyes?

I think because it's not something God will force on us. He won't zap us and make us believe, as if we were robots. No, faith—though built and stoked and aroused by God's work in us, drawing us to himself and encouraging us through the Spirit—is still an utterly human reaction to a situation. Some people exercise it, and some don't. Some just walk away in indifference.

But the ones who truly believe—like this centurion—are always a wonder. The angels themselves rejoice when a human gives that little spark of belief a firm blow and sends it into full flame by proclaiming faith in Jesus.

Jesus is never blasé about such things as faith in him. He never shrugs off a fervent believer as though they were insignificant.

No, Jesus, because he was a complete human himself, is amazed when we believe in him enough to trust him with our lives and the lives of those near and dear to us. He sits back and smiles, I'll bet, and shakes his head a little like a fisherman looking at his prize trout. "Yup, this one's a keeper," he might say, and then turn to the Father and the Holy Spirit and add, "Take a look at this one, guys. He'll really blow you away!"

55

Jesus could have been a great Jewish mother: he was always FEEDING people.

While I was growing up, my best friend was Jewish, and boy, did I love going to his house. Mrs. Tomar always had the best food, and I could count on getting a lot of it when I stopped by.

For some reason, Jews throughout the ages have had a reputation for enjoying good food, and it seems Jesus was no different. On at least three occasions (perhaps more not recorded in the Gospels), Jesus fed the people around him.

The first incident happened when Jesus tried to get away with his disciples for some needed rest. They rowed out onto the water in a boat, but people recognized them, and when they landed at their destination, they found a huge crowd waiting (see Matthew 14:13–21; Mark 6:30–44; Luke 9:10–17; John 6:5–13). The crowd numbered five thousand men. In the typical way of counting a crowd in that culture, only men were numbered, but that means there may have been as many as twenty thousand people when you figure in women and children. The disciples estimated that it would take eight months of one man's wages to feed them all, yet Jesus fed them by using a little boy's scant lunch.

Matthew and Mark both record another incident of miraculous multiplication of fish and bread (Matthew 15:32–39; Mark 8:1–9). Once again, Jesus took what was available—seven small loaves of bread and a few fish—and multiplied it to fill the stomachs of probably four thousand men—likely ten to fifteen thousand people in all.

The last instance in the New Testament of Jesus feeding someone occurred after he rose from the dead. Seven disciples had gone off fishing, perhaps because they needed to do something normal after all the craziness of the crucifixion and resurrection (see John 21:1–14). Jesus appeared on the shore and hailed them. The disciples didn't know it was Jesus, and they'd caught nothing that night. But Jesus told them to cast their nets on the right side of the boat.

Think about it. These fisherman had probably fished from every side of the boat there was. They'd gone in and out, rowed this way and that way, and still caught nothing. Now some guy on shore was telling them to try on "the right side of the boat"? They'd probably tried that a hundred times by now. But they did it anyway, and suddenly they had a huge catch. Undoubtedly it reminded them of a time years earlier, at the start of Jesus's ministry, when a similar command netted a similar miraculous catch of fish when Jesus called them to fish for men.

That's when they realized it was Jesus. Peter jumped into the water and swam to shore while the others rowed the hundred yards or so. They found Jesus cooking fish over a fire. Jesus told them to grab some more fish from their catch (John said there were 153 fish) and invited them to have some breakfast.

Jesus had only recently risen from the dead. The greatest event in the history of the world had just happened. You'd think Jesus would have made some grand pronouncement or something, but lo and behold, it was just a little lunch for the bunch.

How Godlike to be concerned about physical needs when he knew people's focus on the spiritual would take a backseat to a gnawing in the stomach. We see this in the Old Testament with the feeding of the Israelites in the wilderness, the ravens bringing food to Elijah, and the miraculous provision of food for the widow of Zarephath (see 1 Kings 17). The God who created us knows all too well that if we have a real physical need, whether it's food, shelter, or a health issue, often that need must be met first before he can bring our attention to the more important spiritual matters.

Missionaries have taken this cue in reaching out to people with the gospel as well. Many times it's not the preachers who make the first contacts but the doctors who bring desperately needed treatment or the teachers who show people how to raise crops and start businesses.

While some criticize Christianity today for its teachings, the truth is that many people come to Christ first through a loving contact and provision that leads them to ask the question, "Why have you helped me like this?" That's the perfect moment to tell them about our deeper motivation: the Jesus who first showed us real love too.

56

Jesus walked on water, but he had a hard time TEACHING Peter how to do the same.

Most people have heard about Jesus walking on water. It's recorded in the Gospels of Matthew (14:22–34), Mark (6:45–51), and John (6:16–21). Jesus had sent his disciples to cross the Sea of Galilee ahead of him while he dismissed the crowd (after feeding the five thousand) and then went up on a mountainside to pray alone. When night came, the disciples were still rowing, buffeted by the wind and waves beating against the boat. Between three and six a.m. (by Roman reckoning the fourth watch of the night), Jesus walked out on the water to the boat. When the disciples saw a figure walking toward them, they were terrified and cried out in fear—understandable since they thought they were seeing a ghost. Jesus immediately reassured them, saying, "Take courage! It is I. Don't be afraid" (Matthew 14:27).

Peter, always the bold one, and perhaps afraid Jesus would pass them by and wanting to be with him rather than in the slow-moving boat, asked Jesus for something truly startling: "Lord, if it's you," Peter replied, "tell me to come to you on the water" (Matthew 14:28).

Jesus answered, "Come."

"Then Peter got down out of the boat, walked on the water and came toward Jesus. But when he saw the wind, he was afraid and, beginning to sink, cried out, 'Lord, save me!'" (Matthew 14:29).

Jesus immediately reached out and grabbed him, then said, "You of little faith . . . why did you doubt?" (Matthew 14:31).

The disciples were so astonished at this event that when Jesus and Peter climbed back into the boat, they worshiped Jesus, saying, "Truly you are the Son of God" (Matthew 14:33).

What went wrong with Peter? It seems he simply took his eyes off Jesus and focused instead on the violent wind and the waves. As long as he looked to Jesus and fixed his eyes on the Savior, Peter was all right. Perhaps the problem started when he realized what was really happening: he was walking on water, like Jesus. He'd never seen anything like this before. What he was doing was humanly impossible. If he should slip beneath the angry waves, he'd drown for sure. What had he been thinking to ask to walk on water? So he doubted. The immensity of his situation overwhelmed him.

But Jesus came to his rescue. Afterward, all Jesus asked was, "Why did you doubt, Peter?" As if at that point in his spiritual growth, Peter should have known better.

Yet most of us can identify with Peter. When circumstances overwhelm us, we cry out things like, "Where are you, God?" or, "What are you doing to me?"

And how does God respond? He reaches down and rescues us, just as Jesus did for Peter. Later he may gently confront us about our doubt, but it's really more of a learning opportunity than a rebuke. He reminds us that if we just keep our eyes on him, we'll be fine.

When you get into tough straits again, remember Peter and cry out, "Save me, Lord!" It's a short prayer. But also an effective one.

57

Even Jesus PAID taxes.

Ever get angry over your latest tax return? Or the sales tax in your state? Or the tolls on major highways?

Jesus gave one simple command about taxes: pay them.

If anyone should have been exempt from paying taxes, it was Jesus. The Son of God. Owner of the universe. From the most royal family in history. Who would dare demand that Jesus pay taxes to something as fickle and slimy as a government, especially the Roman Empire?

But Jesus did pay taxes. He was as human as us, and he submitted to the laws of human institutions. He didn't flinch or hesitate about it. How he did it, though, is remarkable.

One day some tax collectors cornered Peter and asked him whether Jesus was paying his due. Among Jews, paying taxes ranked as one of the most controversial issues of the century. They not only considered it an act of disobedience to God to pay taxes to a pagan empire, but the very money they paid with was marked by the image of Caesar, which they said constituted a kind of idolatry. Thus, Jews debated daily about paying taxes. So the collectors asked, "Does Jesus pay up or not?"

Here's the story as recorded in Matthew:

After Jesus and his disciples arrived in Capernaum, the collectors of the two-drachma tax came to Peter and asked, "Doesn't your teacher pay the temple tax?"

"Yes, he does," he replied.

When Peter came into the house, Jesus was the first to speak. "What do you think, Simon?" he asked. "From whom do the kings of the earth collect duty and taxes—from their own sons or from others?"

"From others," Peter answered.

"Then the sons are exempt," Jesus said to him. "But so that we may not offend them, go to the lake and throw out your line. Take the first fish you catch; open its mouth and you will find a four-drachma coin. Take it and give it to them for my tax and yours." (Matthew 17:24–27)

Peter obeyed, caught the fish, and presumably paid the tax collectors with the two coins he found in the fish's mouth. This tax on Jews was equal to about two whole days' pay for a workman in Jesus's time.

Today you can catch a fish from the Sea of Galilee called St. Peter's Fish—which, because of its large mouth (where it carries its eggs), could hold a couple of coins the size of the poll tax. Too bad taxes aren't this easy to pay today!

We could ask the question: why did Jesus pay taxes this way—through a miracle of catching a fish? I think there's more reason here than just the fact that Jesus likely had little of his own money and probably couldn't pay it himself. I believe it's an example of hard work combined with supernatural help. If we work honestly and do our part (Peter had to go and catch the fish), God will supernaturally supply us with what we need to pay our taxes. We needn't cheat or fudge or complain. God will always be there for us when we proceed faithfully, and in faith.

This miraculous story teaches a practical lesson. Jesus is telling us, "I understand your problem. Trust me, and I'll get you what you need."

58

Jesus SPAT on a blind man.

Most of Jesus's miracles were rather straightforward. People came to Jesus, asked him to heal them, and Jesus did so. Immediately the blind man saw, the deaf man heard, the lame walked, and the dead arose.

But two miracles stand out as positively weird. The first is recorded in Mark 8:22–26. People from the city of Bethsaida brought a blind man and begged Jesus to heal him. The first uncharacteristic thing Jesus did was to take the man by the hand and lead him out of the village. Then he spit on the man's eyes, put his hands on him (the laying on of hands as for prayer or healing), and said, "Do you see anything?"

The man replied, "I see people; they look like trees walking around."

Jesus placed his hands on the man's eyes one more time. This time his eyes were opened, and he could see everything clearly. Then Jesus sent him home, saying, "Don't go into the village."

Why all these theatrics, and what was wrong with that village? As for the spittle, that's a mystery. Maybe Jesus just wanted to do this one a little differently. Maybe he felt a tad bored and decided to perform a miracle with a little twist. We're not told any special reason for Jesus's healing this way, but we can be sure what he did was exactly right for that situation.

The problem with Bethsaida, the village in question, is that Jesus had denounced it sometime before. Matthew 11:20–24 tells us that Jesus "began to denounce the cities in which most of his miracles had been performed, because they did not repent. 'Woe to you, Korazin! Woe to you, Bethsaida! If the miracles that were performed in you had been performed in Tyre and Sidon, they would have repented long ago in sackcloth and ashes. But I tell you, it will be more bearable for Tyre and Sidon on the day of judgment than for you.'"

Perhaps this man was a newcomer and Jesus didn't want him to be affected by the populace of the city. Maybe with his healing, he also had to find a new home. Regardless, the point is that Jesus knew what had to be done to help this man succeed as a newly sighted person. Jesus healed the man's eyes and then told him what his next step should be.

Through this account we see an example of what happens when Jesus works in our hearts for healing or spiritual change. He lets us know his will through his Word, through our spirits, through others, and through circumstances. He will lead you in the same way. Never despair when you're unsure of your direction. Jesus will show you the way.

59

Jesus's enemies laid MANY traps.

The religious leaders hated Jesus so much that they were bent on catching him in a serious theological mistake. So they began setting traps in order to implicate him in some way that would get him into trouble with the populace—or the authorities—and make getting rid of him that much easier.

The first time they tried this is recorded in John 8:1–11. Some have argued that since this passage is not found in some of the earliest Greek manuscripts of the book of John that it should be excluded from the New Testament. That's for more learned men than I to argue. But the story smacks so much of the character of Jesus and his way of dealing with trouble that most admit it happened.

Let's look at the story.

Jesus had been teaching in the temple. His identity had been repeatedly called into question, but Jesus had answered the leaders straightforwardly. This just infuriated them all the more. The next day Jesus returned to the temple and sat down to teach in one of the temple courts. Before he got going, though, some Pharisees and "teachers of the Law" brought in a woman they had caught in the act of adultery. (By the way, where was the man?) Some believe that rather than acting from motives of righteous regard for the Law, they had set up the woman deliberately and brought her to Jesus to place him in a no-win situation and thus incriminate him.

The leaders made her stand in front of Jesus and then said, "Teacher, this woman was caught in the act of adultery. In the Law Moses commanded us to stone such women. Now what do you say?" (John 8:4–5).

John himself said this was a trap, but how so? It was subtle, but this was the dilemma: the Law said to stone such women. Yet Jesus repeatedly preached about compassion, mercy, and kindness toward your neighbors. So which way would he go? If he said, "Stone her," he was in line with the Law, but only a Roman court could award a verdict for execution. So if he said that, he probably would be in trouble with the Romans. However, if Jesus let her go in the name of mercy, he would be in violation of the Law and thus a heretic. Either way, the leaders figured they had him. Whatever he said, he'd be in trouble with someone important.

Instead of answering their question immediately, John tells us Jesus bent down and wrote on the ground with his finger. What did he write? We don't know. They continued questioning him, so after he finished writing, he said to them, "If any one of you is without sin, let him be the first to throw a stone at her" (John 8:7).

Wow! With one fell swoop, he confirmed both the truth of the law and the spirit of his message of mercy and grace. He had it both ways— and he accomplished a third thing: he confronted the leaders about their own sin. For who could claim to be without any sin at all? Apparently, not even one of these self-righteous hypocrites.

At that point, as the Pharisees and teachers of the Law stood trying to figure out what to do, Jesus stooped and wrote again in the dust. Some commentators believe he wrote words connected to sin. *Thief. Drunkard. Adulterer. Liar.* With each word, they suggest, his eyes may have met those of a person to whom that title applied.

Slowly, one by one, the Jews dropped their stones and headed for the hills.

In the end Jesus was left with just the woman standing there in front of him. He said to her, "Woman, where are they? Has no one condemned you?" (John 8:10).

She shook her head. "No one, sir."

"Then neither do I condemn you," Jesus declared. "Go now and leave your life of sin" (John 8:11).

What a scene! Jesus eluded their trap, confronted them about their own sinfulness, and showed grace and mercy to this sinful woman. How could he pull it off?

Because we're not dealing with just a man but with God himself.

60

Jesus found WAYS to win in unwinnable situations.

The religious leaders foisted a second trap on Jesus, recorded in Mark 12:13–17. This time the sinister elements of the trap were even greater, because the religious Jews brought some of the Herodians—those loyal to King Herod and to Rome—with them. These people had enough powerful influence to get Jesus thrown into jail immediately if they spotted an infraction or rebellion against the Roman government.

What was the issue? Perhaps Israel's greatest beef with Rome: taxes. For many Jews the issue of paying taxes to Caesar brought all kinds of moral and ethical dilemmas. For one thing, they believed God was their real king; therefore, they should pay taxes only to him. For another, Caesar's face was printed on the Roman coins required for paying taxes—coins of bronze, silver, and gold. Since the Romans considered Caesar a god on earth, his image, to a Jew, was considered an idol. The coins were actually inscribed with the words, "Tiberius Caesar Augustus, son of the divine Augustus." To use such money was believed to be a violation of the first and second commandments: "You shall have no other gods before me" (Exodus 20:3) and "You shall not make for yourself an idol in the form of anything in heaven above or on the earth beneath" (Exodus 20:4).

A third problem was with what was known as the "poll tax." This was an annual fee of one denarius (one day's wages). It funded the armies of Rome, who occupied Israel at the time. The intent was to make the people of Israel, who believed they belonged to God alone, feel Rome's claim to lordship over them. For the Jews this was the most egregious outrage of the tax system. Just the subject stirred strong emotions. No wonder the Jews and Herodians chose this subject to try to trap Jesus again. This, finally, was the fight even Jesus would not be able to win. No matter what he said, he'd be in big trouble. Either the Jews would turn on him if he advocated paying taxes, or the Herodians could get him into deep trouble with the ruling Romans.

Although the Pharisees and Herodians were bitter enemies with opposing loyalties and agendas, they were united in their hatred and fear of Jesus. So these traditional foes joined together to try to bring down the one who threatened their positions of influence. Together they went to Jesus to ask their loaded question, but they started first with words of flattery: "Teacher, we know you are a man of integrity." (This, though they believed he was a blasphemer of the highest order). "You aren't swayed by men, because you pay no attention to who they are; but you teach the way of God in accordance with the truth." Jesus was probably thinking, *All this buildup? They must really have a zinger.* And they did: "Is it right to pay taxes to Caesar or not? Should we pay or shouldn't we?" (Mark 12:14–15).

Can you almost feel the silence as the crowd collectively held its breath? All the Jews knew the arguments, and they vehemently hated the Romans and their taxes. But remember the clincher: the Herodians had been planted in this group too. And that was the trap: if Jesus said no to paying taxes, as any good Jew would, he would please the people; but the Herodians would have the evidence they needed to haul him off as a rebel and jail him. If he said yes to paying taxes, the people would be horrified, and he would lose their support. How could Jesus wriggle out of this one?

He found a way. No question is too tough for Jesus, no situation unwinnable. He recognized their hypocrisy and immediately called attention to their real purpose in asking the question: "Why are you trying to trap me?" And then said, "Bring me a denarius and let me look at it" (Mark 12:15).

Someone brought the coin as the whole assembly watched closely, wondering what this was all about. Jesus examined the coin, then held it up for all to see. "Whose portrait is this? And whose inscription?" (Mark 12:16).

"Caesar's," came the reply.

Then Jesus announced his verdict: "Give to Caesar what is Caesar's and to God what is God's" (Mark 12:17).

A knockout punch! With a single sentence, Jesus upheld the Roman law and the Jews' desire for God's exaltation. He showed that obligations to civil authorities didn't have to transgress obligations to God, while at the same time distinguishing clearly between Caesar and God, thus discounting the emperor's claim to deity.

Again Jesus had foiled their entrapment and made hash of their arguments. He not only settled the question of the day, he settled the problem of the century, maybe the millennia. He had won a fight designed to be impossible to win.

The only problem with winning is that it often makes the losers even more angry and determined to beat you. So even though they'd been bested repeatedly, Jesus's enemies weren't ready to throw in the towel. They would come back with more difficult traps. After all, no one could win them all . . . could he?

61

Jesus saw through phony questions and gave REAL answers.

So far the Pharisees and Herodians had taken their shots at trapping Jesus with trick questions they thought had no right answers, but they had failed miserably. Now it was the shrewder, craftier Sadducees' turn. Perhaps they decided they could no longer let the little guys handle Jesus. The question they asked Jesus didn't seem designed to trap him but merely to condescend and make him look foolish.

The Sadducees were the ruling class of Jews who controlled the Sanhedrin, the leading Jewish political assembly. They were wealthy and powerful . . . and also quite deadly. Cross a Sadducee and you had an enemy for life. They didn't believe in angels or the resurrection of the dead, and they only recognized the first five books of the Old Testament, the books of Moses called the Law.

Mark 12:18–27 records the Sadducees' going to Jesus to ask him another question. "Teacher," they said, "Moses wrote for us that if a man's brother dies and leaves a wife but no children, the man must marry the widow and have children for his brother. [This referred to a law from Deuteronomy 25:5–10.] Now there were seven brothers. [This is where it gets fictional. The Jewish teachers loved proposing such problems the same way eighth-graders do with their Sunday-school teachers]. The first one married and died without leaving any children. The second one married the widow, and he also died, leaving no child. It was the same with the third. [Where did they get this story—some wise guy in Hebrew school?] In fact, none of the seven left any children. Last of all, the woman died too. [No small wonder about that.] At the resurrection whose wife will she be, since the seven were married to her?" (Mark 12:19–23).

What was the dilemma? Well, if Jesus said the woman would be married to the first guy in heaven, or something like that, the Sadducees could argue that the story exposed the whole fallacy of the resurrection because it appeared to be an arbitrary answer on the part of God. Why the first one? What if the second husband was nicer to her, and she preferred him? Or what if she really liked two of them, but not the other five? Didn't she get some choice in this matter?

You can see the conundrums that result with such a question, which in the minds of the Sadducees exposed the kinds of difficulties a resurrection theology raised. If one accepts the idea of eternal life in heaven, what determines which people get into heaven in the first place? Good works? How many? And what about the people's sins? What about the sacrifices? What about riches and contributions to earthly life? How were those things rewarded in heaven? Not to mention the whole issue of what kind of body one would receive in heaven. What happened if your body had decayed in the ground? How would God piece you back together?

All these kinds of questions and more were what made the resurrection seem absurd to the Sadducees.

Still, this was a different kind of question from the previous attempts at trapping Jesus in a serious sin, which could have gotten him in trouble with the Roman authorities. Rather, this was more of a theological, rhetorical question that the people constantly debated among themselves and which would lead to Jesus supporting one of two theological camps and dividing his followers—or at least the Pharisees and Sadducees. Each was a small group in terms of numbers, but they were the leaders of the people, wielding tremendous influence over the Jewish population and even the Roman government. It's possible these leaders thought that in humiliating Jesus by stumping him with an unanswerable question, they would make him look foolish and unfit for leadership.

The Sadducees also thought they had an airtight argument. They believed only in the first five books of the Old Testament, which contain no mention of a resurrection or a life after death. So they thought they'd gotten the best of Jesus.

But Jesus didn't flinch. He launched into an answer as if it were so obvious that anyone would have thought of it, even though none of those present had. He said, "Are you not in error because you do not know the Scriptures or the power of God?" (Mark 12:24).

Whoa! Direct shot to the jaw there. Jesus was talking to people who prided themselves not only on how well they knew the Scriptures but also on how well they knew God. He went on: "When the dead rise, they will neither marry nor be given in marriage; they will be like the angels in heaven" (Mark 12:25). (Uh-oh: angels. Now he'd done it. The Sadducees didn't believe in those either. They must have been seething.)

Then Jesus addressed the real crux of their question. They had not come to quibble about whether husband number one, three, or six had the greater claim to the woman in heaven. The real issue was that the Sadducees didn't believe in the resurrection of the dead. If something wasn't specifically mentioned or taught in Genesis through Deuteronomy, the Sadducees rejected it; and life after death simply wasn't covered. Nothing Jesus could say would ever change that.

But Jesus wasn't going to step around the elephant in the room. He confronted it head on, and even though the Sadducees never asked a real question, Jesus gave them real answers—and he gave them answers they couldn't refute. "Now about the dead rising—have you not read in the book of Moses, in the account of the bush [that, by the way, is in the book of Exodus, one of the books the Sadducees proudly believed in], how God said to him, 'I am the God of Abraham, the God of Isaac, and the God of Jacob'? He is not the God of the dead, but of the living. You are badly mistaken" (Mark 12:26–27).

Matthew 12:34 tells us that Jesus's response effectively silenced the Sadducees. Guess they'd underestimated him. From the one part of the Old Testament they accepted and believed, Jesus had just shown them a reference to the resurrection—something they had never accepted or believed. The Sadducees were taught an embarrassing public lesson: don't ask Jesus phony questions if you're not prepared for some real answers.

62

Jesus reduced all of the Law to TWO commandments.

Can he do that? Even though he's God? OK, Jesus didn't really toss out eight commandments. But in response to another test question from an expert in the Law, Jesus did single out one command as being of the highest importance, and a second that was right up there in terms of priority. Which ones merited special mention by Jesus? The first of the Ten Commandments, about having no other gods before the real God? Or the fourth one, about keeping the Sabbath, maybe? Or possibly the fifth commandment, concerning honoring parents? Surely the most important commandment was one of the ten.

But it wasn't.

When Jesus silenced the Sadducees with his proof of the resurrection from the book of Exodus, the Pharisees got back into action (see Matthew 22:34–40). They chose an expert in the Law to test him one more time. This fellow asked, "Teacher, [note that they all start off with this respectful term, even though they all thought Jesus was little more than a country bumpkin] which is the greatest commandment in the Law?"

This was an issue hotly debated by the teachers and scribes. In studying the Old Testament, the rabbis had identified 613 commandments, some of which they classified as lighter and some they considered heavy, or more important. Of these laws, 248 were positive, 365 were negative, and all were mandatory for any observant Jew. However, as to which commandment was the heaviest, or most important, no one could agree.

If Jesus took a stand on one of these or another, he might further alienate people following him who disagreed. But such arguments were beyond the interest and concern of most ordinary Jews. Perhaps the real reason for asking this question was merely to get Jesus to follow the Pharisees down a rabbit trail of endless arguments over "safe," inconsequential subjects instead of authoritatively teaching about the kingdom of heaven and casting out demons. If they couldn't show Jesus's ignorance, back him into a corner, or best him intellectually or spiritually, perhaps they could at least drag him into a never-ending debate—an arena in which the Pharisees particularly excelled.

Jesus answered this expert, "'Love the Lord your God with all your heart and with all your soul and with all your mind.' This is the first and greatest commandment. And the second is like it: 'Love your neighbor as yourself.' All the Law and the Prophets hang on these two commandments" (Matthew 22:37–40).

The account in Mark 12:32–33 includes a further exchange: "Well said, teacher," the man replied. "You are right in saying that God is one and there is no other but him. To love him with all your heart, with all your understanding and with all your strength, and to love your neighbor as yourself is more important than all burnt offerings and sacrifices."

Apparently the man was more open-minded and sincere than the Pharisees who had sent him. Jesus saw that this man had answered wisely, and commended him: "You are not far from the kingdom of God" (Mark 12:34).

Mark wraps it up: "And from then on no one dared ask him any more questions." It's easy to see why, isn't it?

63

Jesus didn't get sidetracked by CONTROVERSY—even when it was about him.

We don't know precisely what the disciples or anyone else believed about Jesus's birth during his time on earth. Perhaps they only learned the truth when Mary divulged the details to Luke, who probably interviewed her about Jesus's early years to write the first few chapters of his gospel, that Jesus was conceived before Mary and Joseph were married.

But we do have one indication that Jesus's enemies knew something about the controversial circumstances surrounding his birth. In one of the many arguments Jesus had with the Pharisees, Jesus told them their father was the devil, the "Father of lies." The Jews retorted that Abraham was their father, not the devil; but Jesus replied that if they truly were children of Abraham (spiritually speaking), they wouldn't try to kill him, because Abraham foresaw Jesus's day and rejoiced in it. The Jews then gave this cryptic retort: "We are not illegitimate children" (John 8:41).

Why did they raise this issue? Perhaps because they believed that was precisely the way Jesus got his own start in our world.

When I was in college, one of our religion professors informed us with passion and eloquence that Jesus could not have been born of a virgin; that was biologically impossible. "No," he said with a gleam in his eye, "Mary probably met some sharp Roman soldier, had a tryst with him, and then made up the story to cover her infidelity to Joseph."

The Bible clearly contradicts such beliefs, yet it's common today for people to think the virgin birth is little more than a hokey story. In the Jewish Talmud, in fact, we can find that very explanation, about a Roman soldier and Mary, repeated and commented on by various rabbis.

Perhaps what's most astonishing is that when the Pharisees made their snide remark, Jesus—as usual—chose not to defend himself against their taunts and accusations. He refused to enter into an argument about rumors and gossip but instead confronted the real issue: that because they'd rejected Jesus, they didn't belong to God.

Come to think of it, why did Jesus so rarely respond to criticism of himself? I think it has much to do with his basic understanding of human nature. Jesus knew the truth, and he also knew these people wouldn't accept the truth. So why argue? Let them persist in their foolishness. The truth will be made clear at the right time, when every nasty mouth is closed, never to be opened again.

God is always patient because he knows the end from the beginning. Troublesome middles never worry him.

64

Jesus put MUD in a blind man's eyes.

An unusual healing is described in John 9:1–12. A discussion arose among the disciples about a blind man they passed on the road. The disciples asked, "Who sinned, this man or his parents, that he was born blind?" And Jesus gave them an unexpected answer: "Neither this man nor his parents sinned," said Jesus, "but this happened so that the work of God might be displayed in his life" (John 9:3). Then, without the blind man's actually asking to be healed, Jesus "spit on the ground, made some mud with the saliva, and put it on the man's eyes. 'Go,' he told him, 'wash in the Pool of Siloam' (this word means "sent"). So the man went and washed, and came home seeing" (John 9:6–7).

Again we have a situation with a few variations on the *normal* miracle. Jesus made a little mud from spittle and dirt, put it on the man's eyes, then told him to wash in a local pool. Why did Jesus have him do these things?

Of course, no one knows the mind of Jesus except God. But some hints come to mind. First, this man had been blind since birth. He may not have had eyes at all (although the passage says Jesus put the mud on his eyes), or they may have been so damaged that they could not be healed in the usual sense. You may remember that in the book of Genesis, God created Adam out of the clay of the ground. Perhaps in this case

Jesus put mud on this man's eyes to miraculously create a whole new pair of eyes.

The Pool of Siloam has no particular significance. The word *siloam* means "sent," and the pool was located southeast of Jerusalem. The water came through a channel that had been dug all the way to the spring of Gihon in the Kidron Valley. The one significant factor here is that the water drawn for the Feast of Tabernacles, in which the Jews commemorated the days when they dwelled in tents after being delivered from bondage in Egypt, came from this pool.

The one thing we know for sure is that Jesus often broke the mold. He never turned his miracles into an assembly-line process. They were personal and unique, and a person could remember his encounter with Jesus with the delicious feeling that Jesus had particularly chosen him.

65

Jesus refuted the concept of KARMA.

The Hindu "Law of Karma" has been around for thousands of years. It states that a person experiences punishments or rewards in his present life on the basis of his previous life. If a person committed murder and all manner of mayhem in a previous life, he might be born crippled, be murdered himself, or some such thing in the present life. If, on the other hand, he was a do-gooder and one who loved people, in his next life he might be born into a high-caste family with wealth, fortune, and all the good things life can bestow.

The problem with the Law of Karma is that it means we get in this life what we deserve. Thus, according to the teachings about Karma, people with diseases, tragedies, and other problems in their lives today are only experiencing the just consequences of what they did in previous lives. Even today in India it's hard to get people to care about the poor, needy, and indigent because they believe they're getting what they deserve according to the Law of Karma. Messing with karma's justice by helping out the unfortunate might even cause one to earn a worse life next time around.

While there's no indication of Indian or Hindu influence in the New Testament, on one occasion Jesus confronted the idea behind the Law of Karma. It's recorded in John 9:1–5. Jesus and his disciples were walking along, talking, when they spotted a blind man, perhaps begging on the side of the road. For some reason they knew the man had been blind since his birth. The disciples asked Jesus, "Who sinned, this man or his parents, that he was born blind?" (John 9:2).

It's the classic theory of karma. Surely this man must have done something wrong to deserve being blind. But it was also a typical way of thinking for Jews of that day. Throughout the Old Testament, in many places God spoke of the consequences for sin. If you sinned, you risked losing much.

The disciples saw only two possibilities for the man's suffering: either his parents had sinned or the man himself had, perhaps in some previous time or place. The Jews didn't believe in reincarnation—they believe we're born once, and after we die, we face God's judgment. But the substance of the disciples' question sounds perilously close to the Law of Karma. Someone must have done something bad for this misfortune to happen to the man.

Jesus immediately stomped all over that theory: "Neither this man nor his parents sinned," said Jesus, "but this happened so that the work of God might be displayed in his life" (John 9:3).

We might be tempted to think all kinds of unkind things about people who suffer. We might even believe they've done something wrong to deserve what they've gotten. Paul even supports that principle in 1 Corinthians 11:29–30, referring to eating the Lord's Supper with sin in your life. He said, "Anyone who eats and drinks without recognizing the body of the Lord eats and drinks judgment on himself. That is why many among you are weak and sick, and a number of you have fallen asleep." Clearly Paul believed that taking communion in a dishonorable way invited God's wrath.

But this is not the same principle as that concerning the blind man. For calamities that seem to have no explanation, Jesus offered one: this person's problem will display God's work and glory.

Any problem or trial can be used by God to glorify himself through that person's good attitude, through his doing of good despite his problem, and so on. It might even be an opportunity for a miracle, which God still does, even today.

The Law of Karma is a hopeless, meanspirited explanation for why people suffer. Yes, there are consequences of sin. An alcoholic invites illness on many fronts. A sexual deviant can contract disease. But in many cases the reason for suffering is not that the person sinned. And while we may not have all the answers, we have the one that counts: God can do something great in that person.

66

Jesus faced down SEVERAL murderous mobs.

While the Italian mafia probably didn't exist in Jesus's day, plenty of mobs were around with murder in mind. Several times before his actual death on the cross, Jesus faced down people who wanted to do him in.

The first incident happened in his hometown. Jesus spoke in the synagogue in Nazareth, reading a text from Isaiah 61:1–2 and stating that it had been fulfilled in their hearing. The people seemed excited about this until Jesus began to preach, telling them that no prophet was ever accepted in his hometown and then referring to the case of Elijah. But he didn't show how Elijah's hometown had rejected him. No, he preached about how Elijah had ministered only to foreigners (Gentiles) and gave the suggestion that perhaps the reason Jews didn't get this outpouring of grace was because they had put down their prophets.

This incited the crowd, and they drove Jesus out to the edge of town, where they tried to cast him off a cliff. But Jesus simply walked through the crowd, passing by the angry townies and miraculously walking away unharmed (see Luke 4:28–30).

The second incident is recorded in John 5. Jesus healed a man on the Sabbath, and when he explained to the Jewish people why he did it, he said, "My Father is always at his work to this very day, and I, too, am working" (John 5:17). When the Jews heard this, they "tried all the harder to kill him;

not only was he breaking the Sabbath, but he was even calling God his own Father, making himself equal with God" (John 5:18). While we don't know precisely what action they took at that point to work toward Jesus's death (this happened early in his ministry), they certainly didn't think years would pass before their chance would come. It's realistic to think they went away that afternoon to discuss what they could do to put him away.

Usually these fits of anger and hatred came when Jesus said something potent and riling—like the event in his hometown and later his claiming to be equal with God. It was the truth, but the Jews considered it blasphemy—the worst sin of all.

John 7 tells of a third incident, when Jesus traveled to Jerusalem for the Feast of Tabernacles—even though he knew the Jewish leaders there were seeking to kill him. During the feast Jesus did some teaching in the temple courts, and the people were intrigued. Everyone was talking about him, trying to figure out what to make of him. "Isn't this the man they are trying to kill? Here he is, speaking publicly, and they are not saying a word to him. Have the authorities really concluded that he is the Christ? But we know where this man is from; when the Christ comes, no one will know where he is from" (John 7:25–27).

Jesus replied to this, "Yes, you know me, and you know where I am from." [More hometown problems.] "I am not here on my own, but he who sent me is true. You do not know him, but I know him because I am from him and he sent me" (John 7:28–29).

This ignited the crowd, and "they tried to seize him, but no one laid a hand on him, because his time had not yet come" (John 7:30). Once again a mob was thwarted by God's miraculous protection of Jesus.

The last situation came about at the Feast of Dedication in Jerusalem:

It was winter, and Jesus was in the temple area walking in Solomon's Colonnade. The Jews gathered around him, saying, "How long will you keep us in suspense? If you are the Christ, tell us plainly."

Jesus answered, "I did tell you, but you do not believe. The miracles I do in my Father's name speak for me, but you do not believe because you are not my sheep. My sheep listen to my voice; I know them, and they follow me. I give them eternal life, and they shall never perish; no one can snatch them out of my hand. My Father, who has given them to me, is greater than all; no one can snatch them out of my Father's hand. I and the Father are one" (John 10:22–30).

Once again the leaders were blinded by murderous rage at Jesus's claims about being equal with God, being at one with him, and claiming to be the Son of God.

What happened? "Again the crowd picked up stones to stone him, but Jesus said to them, 'I have shown you many great miracles from the Father. For which of these do you stone me?' 'We are not stoning you for any of these,' replied the Jews, 'but for blasphemy, because you, a mere man, claim to be God'" (John 10:31–33).

Jesus didn't back down from his claims but rather gave them more proof: Scripture and the miracles he did. He urged them to "know and understand that the Father is in me, and I in the Father" (John 10:38). But they were beyond reason; they just wanted to destroy Jesus. "Again they tried to seize him, but he escaped their grasp" (John 10:39).

It appears from these episodes that Jesus's life was constantly at risk, not only in a long-term, plotted sense, but in an immediate sense as well. His enemies were ready to do him in whenever they had the opportunity, no questions asked. The main reason Jesus kept running into these confrontations was because he told them the truth—that he is the Son of God, God himself. Nothing infuriated Jewish teachers more than someone standing up and saying, "Hey, I'm God."

Like Jesus you, too, will face people who reject the truth you're speaking to them. They may even attack you, insult you, and hate you. But like Jesus, don't let it bother you. God will protect you, lead you, empower you. As Jesus said in Matthew 10:19, don't worry about what you should say or do. The Holy Spirit in that moment will fill your mind with the words you need, and God will stand with you the same way he stood with his Son, Jesus.

67

Jesus let a good friend DIE.

What would you do if a good friend of yours was dying? Would you rush to his side, especially if his family called for you? What if it were in your power to help him—to heal him, as Jesus could. And what if, in spite of this fact, you stayed where you were for two days—as Jesus did? What kind of friend would you be? What kind of friend was Jesus when he let his friend Lazarus die? Let's find out.

When their brother Lazarus became gravely ill, Mary and Martha sent urgent word to Jesus: "Lord, the one you love is sick" (John 11:3). They probably had no doubt Jesus would know what to do and would come quickly. After all, "Jesus loved Martha and her sister and Lazarus. Yet when he heard that Lazarus was sick, he stayed where he was two more days" (John 11:5–6). What kind of sense does that make?

When the messengers brought word to Jesus, Lazarus probably was already dead. Bethany was a day's journey from where Jesus was—the place across the Jordan River where John had baptized. Instead of rushing to Lazarus's side, Jesus waited two days, then traveled to Bethany, which took one more day. When he arrived, Lazarus had been dead for four days. But Jesus, in his divine omniscience, knew the end from the beginning; he had a purpose for what he was doing.

Jesus told his disciples when he first learned of the problem, "This sickness will not end in death. No, it is for God's glory so that God's Son may be glorified through it" (John 11:4). He understood that raising Lazarus from the dead would bring much honor and acclaim to God the Father and to himself. Later, in John 12:9–11, we learn that many people became followers of Christ as a result of Lazarus's resurrection. So considering the conclusion of the event, it must have been Jesus's intent all along to raise Lazarus from the dead.

But why four days? Why did Jesus wait two days and let the family go through all the grief and agony of wondering why he never showed up?

A traditional Jewish belief at the time was that the spirit of a dead person hovered around the body for four days. After that it left for the afterlife, and resuscitation was impossible. All the other resuscitations in the New Testament occurred shortly after death, but Lazarus's resurrection may have been an attempt by Jesus to show that he truly had power over death—no matter how long a person had been dead. When people saw this resurrection, they believed Jesus had powers that few knew about. They knew then that he was who he said he was. And God was glorified.

Many times God waits to heal, to help, to turn a situation around, to fix a problem. Some people have prayed for years about such things as family difficulties, the salvation of a loved one, a terminal disease. But this passage in John provides one powerful answer to the question of why God sometimes waits: "It is for God's glory so that God's Son may be glorified through it." We may not see that glory right away, or even for a long time; but it will come.

68

Jesus ENDANGERED people's lives.

Jesus is the Prince of Peace who came to save the world. So it would seem those who follow Jesus might expect a peaceful, safe existence, right? Not on your life! Jesus said, "Do not suppose that I have come to bring peace to the earth. I did not come to bring peace, but a sword" (Matthew 10:34). He also said, "All men will hate you because of me, but he who stands firm to the end will be saved" (Matthew 10:22).

We know how hated Jesus was by many of the religious leaders of his day. It's also true that Jesus's followers were at risk from the same hatred: many eventually became martyrs for their faith. But did you know that even some of the people Jesus merely healed also became victims of the hatred?

Lazarus is perhaps the best example of the extreme danger faced by those Jesus healed. John 12:9–11 tells us that large crowds came out to see Lazarus after Jesus raised him from the dead. From that time on the chief priests sought to take away from Lazarus what Jesus had restored: "The chief priests made plans to kill Lazarus as well, for on account of him many of the Jews were going over to Jesus and putting their faith in him" (John 12:10–11). Seems like anything that showed Jesus in a good light cast a shadow on them, and they weren't going to put up with it.

They would try to stifle Jesus's popularity by making it dangerous to be his follower—or even to be a beneficiary of his power and grace.

Another interesting example is the way the religious leaders treated a blind man Jesus healed (see John 9:1–41). After Jesus healed him, a dispute arose among some people as to whether this actually was the same man who had been born blind. Some said, "He only looks like him" (John 9:9). But the healed man insisted he was one and the same.

At that point things started to get rough, for skeptics brought some Pharisees to question the blind man, since Jesus had healed him on the Sabbath day. In response to the former blind man's explanation of all he knew about what had happened to him, some of the Pharisees were quick to denounce Jesus and his kindness to the man: "This man is not from God, for he does not keep the Sabbath" (John 9:16).

But other Pharisees were conflicted. They countered, "How can a sinner do such marvelous signs?" (John 9:16). It seemed an obvious question, and no one could answer it.

They turned back to the healed man and cross-examined him further. This time they wanted more than the facts: they wanted his judgment. "What have you to say about him? It was your eyes he opened." The man replied, "He is a prophet" (John 9:17).

This must have displeased the Pharisees, because they changed tactics. They sent for the man's parents. Can you almost hear the venom in their words in John 9:19? "Is this the one you say was born blind? How is it that now he can see?" The pressure of their intimidation tactics is obvious in the response of the man's parents: "We know he is our son," the parents answered, "and we know he was born blind. But how he can see now, or who opened his eyes, we don't know. Ask him. He is of age; he will speak for himself" (John 9:20–21).

John 9:22 explains why the parents were so eager to avoid getting involved beyond giving the barest essential facts: "His parents said this because they were afraid of the Jews, for already the Jews had decided that anyone who acknowledged that Jesus was the Christ would be put out of the synagogue." The intimidated parents just wanted to stay out of it. So far so good. Then they called the blind man back again and pushed him to denounce the man who had healed him. "Give glory to God," they said. "We know this man is a sinner" (John 9:24).

And then this poor guy gave the answer of the century: "Whether he is a sinner or not, I don't know. One thing I do know: I was blind, but now I see!" (John 9:25).

So the Pharisees wanted to hear it all again. How did it happen?

According to John 9:27, the newly sighted man said, "I have told you already and you did not listen" (cannon shot 1). "Why do you want to hear it again? Do you want to become his disciples, too?" (cannon shot 2).

You'd think these apes would have gotten it by now. But no, they roared on, hurling insults (what they considered insults) at the blind man: "You are this fellow's disciple! We are disciples of Moses! We know that God spoke to Moses, but as for this fellow, we don't even know where he comes from." Ah, they admit they're ignoramuses, and they don't even know it.

But here comes cannon shot 3: The man said, "Now that is remarkable! You don't know where he comes from, yet he opened my eyes." Now he would teach these boys some theology they'd apparently missed in Hebrew school. "We know that God does not listen to sinners. He listens to the godly man who does his will." All right, here it comes: "Nobody has ever heard of opening the eyes of a man born blind. If this man were not from God, he could do nothing" (see John 9:30–33). What a theology lesson. Can we get this guy a professorship at some local seminary?

What did the meanspirited leaders do next? When arguments, logic, and reason failed, they got nasty: "You were steeped in sin at birth; how dare you lecture us!" (John 9:34). Then they threw the man out of the synagogue.

It's a powerful picture. A man has been healed, a life turned around, and the response he gets from the powers that be is to be thrown out of the synagogue.

Similarly, we can expect to be hated, perhaps even by some in our own church, when we have a life-transforming encounter with Christ. I've heard of churches excommunicating new Christians out of jealousy, perhaps, and anger at the change in their lives, their enthusiasm for the things of God, and the obvious love they have for Jesus. The "Pharisees" of today, those who believe more in man-made rules than in real faith and grace will react negatively to anyone who displays the real thing.

But that's not the end of the story. John 9:35–38 tells us that Jesus heard about the Pharisees' treatment of the man and sought him out. "Do you believe in the Son of Man?" Jesus asked.

The man replied, "Who is he, sir? Tell me so I may believe in him."

Jesus answered, "You have now seen him," taking him back to his pre-vision days. "In fact, he is the one speaking with you."

The man said, "Lord, I believe," and worshiped him. The guy got his sight back and was saved, all in a matter of hours.

The great news here is that even though you may face rejection from the very community who purported to love you all along, Jesus will be there for you. He'll reassure you, guide you, and give you what you need to get on with real living.

69

Jesus called some RELIGIOUS leaders sons of the devil.

We know the teachers of the Law, scribes, and Pharisees repeatedly accused Jesus of being from the devil. Since they couldn't admit his power came from God, it was the only explanation they could come up with to account for the miracles. After all, no mere human was capable of healing a blind man or raising a dead person. Since they could not countenance the idea that Jesus was the Messiah, God incarnate, the King of kings and Lord of lords, they had to go in the opposite direction. What other supernatural explanation was available? After all, they didn't know about UFOs or possible visitors from outer space; so they were stuck. It was either accept him as God and worship him or accuse him of being the devil and kill him.

Did you know, though, that Jesus turned the tables on these guys and told them point-blank that *they* were children of the devil? You'll find it in John 8:42–47:

> Jesus said to them, "If God were your Father, you would love me, for I came from God and now am here. I have not come on my own; but he sent me. Why is my language not clear to you? Because you are unable to hear what I say. You belong to your father, the devil, and you want to carry out your father's desire. He was a murderer from the beginning, not holding to the truth,

for there is no truth in him. When he lies, he speaks his native language, for he is a liar and the father of lies. Yet because I tell the truth, you do not believe me! Can any of you prove me guilty of sin? If I am telling the truth, why don't you believe me? He who belongs to God hears what God says. The reason you do not hear is that you do not belong to God."

What a scathing indictment! Jesus wrapped it all up in an airtight argument:

1. If they belonged to the living God, they could have no other response to Jesus than to love him and follow him.

2. They didn't seem to understand what Jesus said. Why? Because they were "unable to hear" what he said.

3. Why couldn't they hear? Because they were of their father, the devil. They were doing the devil's work at that very moment.

4. The fact that these people wanted to murder Jesus further reinforced they were sons of the devil, for Satan was a murderer from the start, and they were just like their father. They simply did not know the truth.

5. Why didn't they know the truth? Because they were of the devil, a liar incapable of knowing and embracing any form of truth.

6. How can we know that what Jesus was telling them is true? Simply look at the record: of what sin could they accuse Jesus? None. But still they refused to believe in him.

7. Why is this? For one basic reason: they didn't belong to God. They belonged to the devil and could hear only his lies.

Pretty tight, isn't it? Man, am I glad I wasn't one of those guys. Aren't you?

70

Jesus had powerful
SECRET disciples.

Once, when the leading priests and Pharisees sent temple guards to arrest Jesus, the guards returned without a prisoner and without excuses but with obvious admiration for Jesus. "We have never heard anyone talk like this," they told the Pharisees. "Have you been led astray too?" the Pharisees mocked. "Is there a single one of us rulers or Pharisees who believes in him?" (John 7:46–48 NLT). The answer was supposed to be no, but was it? Actually, a few leaders and Pharisees weren't so quick to judge and actually became followers of Jesus.

In John 3:1–21 we're introduced to the first of these powerful men who were open to Jesus's teaching. Nicodemus was a member of the Sanhedrin, the ruling council, which was made up of some seventy-one members, including scribes, Pharisees, Sadducees, influential family heads, and elders. They carried out civil and religious legal proceedings, although they could not enact capital punishment. Only the Romans could execute those judged criminals.

Nicodemus came to Jesus by night (was he afraid of being seen with Jesus during the daytime?) and asked him a number of questions. The conversation, found in John 3, is a classic of confrontational evangelism, in which a great teacher of Israel was put in his place by a plain-spoken Galilean who revealed some of the greatest truths of the New Testament, including, "You must be born again" (John 3:7), "Just as Moses lifted up the snake in the desert, so the Son of Man must be lifted up, that everyone who believes in him may have eternal life" (John 3:14), and most famous of all, "God so loved the world that he gave his one and only Son, that whoever believes in him shall not perish but have eternal life" (John 3:16).

Nicodemus is not in the picture for most of the recorded ministry of Jesus, but he appears at several crucial junctures. In John 7:45–52, during the incident noted above when the temple guards refused to arrest Jesus and the Pharisees denounced them, ironically, saying none of the Pharisees or religious leaders believed in Jesus, the exception that proved the rule spoke up: "Nicodemus, who had gone to Jesus earlier and who was one of their own number, asked, 'Does our law condemn anyone without first hearing him to find out what he is doing?'" (John 7:50–51).

It must have taken a lot of courage for Nicodemus to defend Jesus as much as he did, for the sentiment against Jesus was strong. His associates replied, "Are you from Galilee, too? Look into it, and you will find that a prophet does not come out of Galilee" (John 7:52).

Nicodemus bided his time until after Jesus's death. Then he and another powerful secret disciple, Joseph of Arimathea, stepped boldly to the forefront when the rest of Jesus's disciples had fled in fear. Joseph was a member of the Sanhedrin and wealthy (see Matthew 27:57). He was a good and upright man who did not consent in the decision of the Sanhedrin to condemn Jesus. Luke describes him as "waiting for the kingdom of God" (Luke 23:51), and apparently he believed he had found it in Jesus.

These two powerful men had been powerless to stop Jesus's crucifixion, but they did what they could for Jesus after his death. Joseph went to Pilate and asked for the Savior's body. This took great courage for a member of the very group that had condemned the Lord. John 19:39 tells us Joseph was accompanied by Nicodemus, who brought seventy-five pounds of myrrh and aloes to anoint and perfume Jesus's body. They wrapped the body in strips of linen, mingling the myrrh and aloes, the Jewish method of preparing a body for burial. The mixture kept down the odor of decay for a time, until the body could be interred. They placed Jesus in Joseph's own new tomb (Matthew 27:59–60).

Nicodemus and Joseph obviously had faith but had kept their faith secret for fear of being put out of the synagogue, a Jewish form of excommunication.

Many other leaders and rulers also believed in Jesus: "Many even among the leaders believed in him. But because of the Pharisees they would not confess their faith for fear that they would be put out of the synagogue; for they loved praise from men more than praise from God" (John 12:42–43). These people would not make a public confession of their faith in Christ for fear of the Pharisees; but public confession is a crucial part of salvation. Romans 10:9–10 says, "If you confess with your mouth, 'Jesus is Lord,' and believe in your heart that God raised him from the dead, you will be saved. For it is with your heart that you believe and are justified, and it is with your mouth that you confess and are saved."

Were these people true Christians? Perhaps not until after the death and resurrection of Jesus, when they finally took a courageous public stand. Or maybe it was on the Day of Pentecost, when Peter preached his remarkable sermon. That day more than three thousand people from Jerusalem believed in Christ, and perhaps among them were these same leaders, emboldened by the power of the indwelling Spirit to make public their statement of faith.

71

Jesus's BLUNTNESS
made people squirm.

We often think of Jesus as the gentle Lamb of God. But he had his moments.

For instance, there's the time he healed the man with the withered hand in Mark 3:1–6. Jesus came into a synagogue and began teaching on the Sabbath. The leading Jews sent up some of their boys to watch Jesus and perhaps catch him healing on the Sabbath, something they believed was evil.

When Jesus saw this man with a shriveled hand, he called him to the front. Then he looked out at the crowd and addressed the critics: "Which is lawful on the Sabbath: to do good or to do evil, to save life or kill?"

I know it's just a simple question, but can you imagine a touch of irritation or a little edge in his voice? Jesus was pretty angry at these nitpicking hypocrites, and it came out in the way the question was phrased.

In Mark 2:1–5 we see another instance. As Jesus was teaching at someone's house, some friends brought a paralytic to him. But there was such a crowd that the friends had to climb up to the roof, dig a hole in it, and let the paralytic down to Jesus. In those days, builders made the roof flat so the owners could sleep there on hot nights or just sit there, enjoying the sights. Slabs of dried clay were laid on beams, and then wet clay was applied to make the surface waterproof. When this man plunked down in front of him, Jesus said to the paralytic, "Son, your sins are forgiven!" Immediately the nitpickers saw an opening. Who could forgive sins but God alone? Was Jesus saying he was God?

Jesus instantly recognized their thoughts and said, perhaps a little abrasively (my rendering), "OK, boys, here's the real issue: which is easier—to say to the paralytic, 'Your sins are forgiven,' or to say, 'Rise, grab your mat, and walk home?'"

Of course, it's pretty easy to *say* someone's sins are forgiven, even if you don't have any authority. The real test is the other part of the challenge, to make someone walk. So Jesus said, in effect, "But just so you naysayers get it, that I have authority on earth to forgive sins, I'll do the one thing none of you can do—I'll make this paralyzed man walk to prove I can forgive sins too." Which is precisely what he did.

In Mark 9:14–32 we read about the time Jesus came down from the Mount of Transfiguration to find his disciples arguing with skeptics and critics. When Jesus asked what was going on, a man who had brought his son to them, asking them to cast out a demon, explained about his son's problem, saying the disciples couldn't cast out the demon. Jesus cried out in frustration, "O unbelieving generation, how long shall I stay with you? How long shall I put up with you? Bring the boy to me." Jesus was fed up, and his words showed it.

Still another occasion in which I think Jesus's directness may have made others uncomfortable is when several people made grandiose promises about following him (see Luke 9:57–62). One told Jesus, "I will follow you wherever you go."

In response Jesus said, "Foxes have holes and birds of the air have nests, but the Son of Man has no place to lay his head." In other words, "Are you sure what you're saying, my friend? You come with me and you'll be homeless and penniless. Have you really taken into account what this is all about?"

Next, a man said, "Lord, first let me go and bury my father." Jesus retorted, "Let the dead bury their own dead, but you go and proclaim the kingdom of God." No delays or excuses allowed; Jesus's call required an unqualified response.

On another occasion, when Jesus healed ten lepers (see Luke 17:11–19), only one came back to thank him. This one happened to be a non-Jew, so when he returned to thank Jesus, the Savior said, "Were not all ten cleansed? Where are the other nine? Was no one found to return and give praise to God except this foreigner?" Rather than gloss over their ingratitude, he brought it front and center.

The case I find most difficult to swallow is recorded in Matthew 15:21–28. A Canaanite woman came to Jesus and pleaded with him to cast a demon out of her daughter. Jesus ignored her until his disciples complained and asked him to send her away. That was when Jesus said to her, "I was sent only to the lost sheep of Israel."

The woman in desperation fell at his feet and cried out, "Lord, help me!"

This time Jesus said, "It is not right to take the children's bread and toss it to their dogs." Frankly, I find this uncharacteristic of Jesus. In fact, the whole situation smacks of bigotry, racism, and qualities we assign to the lowdown creeps of society. We know Jesus was not just sent to Israel, and we also know that he healed all who came to him, whether they were Jews or not. So what was going on here?

I think the Lord's seemingly insensitive remark arose out of a troublesome situation just before this event. Some Pharisees and teachers of the Law had confronted Jesus about his disciples not following the laws about washing their hands before eating. But Jesus turned it around into a tirade against their hypocrisy of not obeying the true Law of Moses rather than all the little rules made up by the rabbis. When even Jesus's disciples still didn't get it, he said, "Are you still so dull?" (see Matthew 15:16). Then he explained the truth about hand-washing and uncleanness. He seemed pretty exasperated at that point, and maybe the burden of pressing crowds, complaining critics, and dense disciples was weighing on him.

Then along came this foreigner begging for his help. Jesus probably longed to find someone who exhibited real faith instead of the grabbing, demanding, "do this for me, me, me" kind of attitude he faced continually. So I honestly think he was testing the woman, maybe being a little tough to see what she would say. (It's worth noting that the word he used for "dogs" is not the Jewish epithet for non-Jews but the word for a family pet, a hint that he meant something different than just an ethnic barb.)

The woman answered brilliantly: "Yes, Lord, but even the dogs eat the crumbs that fall from their master's table" (Matthew 15:27).

Jesus was so impressed that he replied, "Woman, you have great faith! Your request is granted."

There are many other times when Jesus spoke tough words. Yet even his harshest remarks were not meant to wound but to point people toward real healing and hope. I think the tone in some of his comments shows that even he sometimes felt frustrated, like he just wasn't getting through to his listeners. But contrary to others who might just give up or haul off and smack someone "upside the head," Jesus kept trying, repeating the same message, encouraging, and even rebuking. Either way, he told the truth bluntly, even when it didn't go over so well with his hearers.

I find that an endearing trait.

72

Jesus had a sense of HUMOR.

Did Jesus tell jokes? You know, the one about the Pharisee, the Sadducee, and the disciple? Or maybe just a pun now and then? In reality, the gospels are full of examples of Jesus's sense of humor. Take a look at these.

First, in the Sermon on the Mount we find several humorously intended statements. For instance, when Jesus talked about his people being "the light of the world," he said, "People don't light a lamp and put it under a bowl, do they?" (paraphrased from Matthew 5:15). Meaning, of course, such a thing is ridiculous—and I imagine the crowd laughed.

When he spoke of the various ways hypocritical people made public shows of their spirituality by sounding a trumpet when they gave alms, praying on street corners, and letting everyone know they were fasting by neglecting their clothing and wearing a sad face the whole time, Jesus said, "I tell you the truth, they have their reward in full" (Matthew 6:2, 5, 16). The crowd must have smiled at the accurate descriptions, as they'd all seen them carried out in reality.

Speaking about judging others, Jesus told his listeners to take the "planks" out of their own eyes before criticizing others for the "specks of sawdust" in theirs. Again, I think the people must have chuckled at that analogy which so perfectly depicted the hypocrisy of those who judged others.

On another occasion Jesus told his disciples something that just did not compute when the rich young ruler came to him but was turned away because he wouldn't part with his riches. To the disciples (and to many people even today), having riches was a sign of God's blessing and love. But Jesus blew that theory apart when he quipped it was easier "for a camel to go through the eye of a needle than for a rich man to enter the kingdom of God" (Mark 10:25).

Then there was the feeding of the five thousand. When the sun began to set, the disciples advised Jesus to send the crowd away so they could go to the village and get some food (see Matthew 14:13–21). Jesus replied, perhaps with a twinkle in his eye, "They don't need to go away—you give them something to eat."

I suspect the disciples stood there stunned, then glanced at each other and snickered. "Wait a second, Lord. Did I hear you right on that one?" When Jesus stared at them, appearing quite serious but perhaps hiding a slight smile, they informed him they had only five small pieces of bread and two fish. I picture Jesus throwing his hands in the air as he said, "Bring them to me"—the very thing he must have intended all along.

Read through any conversation you find that Jesus had with people, and you'll find him exhibiting real wit. He certainly never attempted real comedy. That would have run counter to the whole tenor of his mission. But I recall listening to an actor recite the gospel of Mark, indicating through inflection the ways Jesus might have said things to be quite witty and at times even humorous.

Probably the primary theater for Jesus's show of humor was at all those dinners with "sinners and tax collectors." They were a rowdy bunch, but they clearly enjoyed Jesus's presence. Though we don't know much of what he said on such occasions, I believe there was much laughter. Jesus must have been an entertaining and interesting guest, or he wouldn't have gotten past the front door. Yes, his spiritual input must have been powerful and a strong draw. But undoubtedly he also knew how to enjoy himself in such company, or they soon would have written him off as just another version of the strict and judgmental Pharisees.

73

Jesus knew how to have FUN.

Solomon said, "There is a time for everything and a season for every activity under heaven: a time to be born and a time to die . . . a time to weep and a time to laugh, a time to mourn and a time to dance" (Ecclesiastes 3:1–2, 4). Psalm 118:24 says, "This is the day the Lord has made; let us rejoice and be glad in it." And Philippians 4:4 tells us, "Rejoice in the Lord always. I will say it again: Rejoice!"

We know Jesus wept. We know he mourned. We even know he danced. (See chapter 82 on the dancing Jesus). But did he ever laugh? Did he ever rejoice so uproariously that he just let go with a real guffaw?

The movie *The Passion of the Christ,* for all its dark themes, portrays Jesus as a fun-maker, a smiler. But was he really? Isaiah told us that he was a "man of sorrows, and familiar with suffering" (Isaiah 53:3). We see him in that way quite often in the New Testament.

But what about a moment of such sheer joy that he slapped Peter on the back and chortled, "Good one, Pete!"

Jesus was called a "drunkard and a glutton." While we have no indication he ever drank to excess or greedily devoured mounds of food, isn't sharing food and drink at a dinner a time of fun and exhilaration? People tell stories and jokes. Others laugh. Can you really imagine Jesus sitting there with a scowl on his face and his arms folded across his chest?

If he was like that, I don't think he would have found himself a guest at such gatherings quite as often.

No, the Scriptures say he was a "friend of tax gatherers and sinners." Don't you think they must have told him a joke or two? "Knock-knock." "Who's there?" "Weed." "Weed who?" "Weed like to hear more about this gospel of yours."

I'm sure any of those sinners and tax collectors who told dirty, lurid, or racist jokes soon felt Jesus's censure. But innocent, funny, cute humor? Why not?

Of course, we don't really know. But I'm not sure I could relate to a Jesus who never laughed. The New Testament never actually says he laughed. Not in those terms.

But joy and rejoicing are considered fruit of the Spirit, and Jesus was filled with the Spirit. So he must have exhibited joy. Any evidence?

Two examples in the Bible make me think Jesus was a man of joy, one who must have laughed at times and enjoyed fellowship, love, goodness, honor, and all those other gifts that make life fulfilling.

First, Zephaniah 3:17 says, "The LORD your God is with you, he is mighty to save. He will take great delight in you, he will quiet you with his love, he will rejoice over you with singing." This is a picture of how God rejoices when we become fully his. Wouldn't Jesus have rejoiced like that when people believed in him, accepted him, loved him?

The second example is from the parable of the prodigal son. The story of the son who took his inheritance and wasted it on wild living is a classic. Eventually he slunk back toward home, bereft of everything, hoping only to become a slave in his father's house. Jesus said, "While he was still a long way off, his father saw him and was filled with compassion for him; he ran to his son, threw his arms around him and kissed him" (Luke 15:20). The father was so excited that he took the signet ring off his finger and put it on the son's finger. He placed a magnificent robe on him and called for a party. When the older son, who had remained loyal all those years, saw this, he was incensed and rejected what his father was doing. But the father explained, "We had to celebrate and be glad, because this brother of yours was dead and is alive again; he was lost and is found" (Luke 15:32).

Clearly, Jesus meant to portray this as the kind of response he and his Father have toward repentant people who come to God for help, friendship, forgiveness, and salvation.

If Jesus never happened to laugh or really rejoice like that while on earth, we can still be sure that he was and is filled with the joy of the Spirit. Every time one of his lost ones finds his or her way back to him, I suspect that Jesus, the Father, and the Spirit all have a rejoicing moment, with the angels dancing and shouting around them. In fact, Jesus said that very thing earlier in Luke 15, through the parables of the lost sheep and the lost coin: "In the same way, I tell you, there is rejoicing in the presence of the angels of God over one sinner who repents" (Luke 15:10).

You may think of Jesus as a dour, preacher sort. But such an image simply does not square with the general tone of Scripture. How could it be filled with so many commands to rejoice (just read the book of Philippians sometime) if Jesus—the Word himself—was not a man of joy? He can make you such a person too, if you'll ask him. And what would appeal more to those we want to reach with the gospel than a joyful heart and manner?

74

Jesus was ACCUSED of being a real party boy.

Believe it or not, many accused Jesus of being the ultimate party boy. Was he?

When we read the stories in the Gospels, we find that when Jesus wasn't healing and teaching, he was eating and drinking with people, sometimes at parties or weddings or lavish dinners.

The first "party" we see him at is in John 2:1–11, when Jesus visited a wedding feast in Cana. There, when the wine ran out, it didn't take much to get him to turn several hundred gallons of water into the best wine the people of that region had ever tasted. Apparently Jesus knew the happily married couple might be humiliated by this social faux pas, so he made sure they had enough.

Some people, of course, didn't much like the fun Jesus had on such occasions. In fact, the Pharisees and legal wits who stood outside the circle of Jesus's friends and carped and complained, then stuck their noses in the air about whom Jesus was dining with, called him a glutton and a drunkard, a friend of tax collectors and sinners (see Matthew 11:19). Presumably, Jesus was more concerned with being a healing and spiritual force in the lives of the people he dined with than about some slur. We never see Jesus drunk in the Bible, and there's also no indication he was actually a glutton.

But when the Pharisees got wind of Jesus's habit of hanging out with the losers, scoundrels, and sinners of the world, they confronted his disciples, asking them, "Why does your teacher eat with tax collectors and 'sinners'?" (see Matthew 9:11). They were not only astonished but infuriated. Why wasn't he eating with *them*? Why didn't he come to *their* banquets? Wasn't their wine good enough for him?

Of course, Jesus did dine in their homes now and then (see Luke 7:36–50). However, when we read that passage, we find that he was insulted: the master of the house didn't even make sure Jesus's feet were washed (a significant slight). Probably, as the Jewish leaders' opposition to Jesus became more oppressive, it just naturally became a stigma for such a person to have Jesus in his home.

When the Pharisees couldn't understand how Jesus could go to a sinner's home and partake as he did, he responded to their slander by saying, "It is not the healthy who need a doctor, but the sick. But go and learn what this means, 'I desire mercy, not sacrifice.' For I have not come to call the righteous, but sinners" (Matthew 9:12–13).

Was Jesus cutting off from his ministrations a very important and powerful part of the population? To some degree, but maybe it was just the law of opposition. You don't tend to spend a lot of time with enemies who seek to kill you, especially when they think they're more righteous and better than everyone else. These guys were proud about their heritage, spirituality, and religious habits. But Jesus called them hypocrites. When you don't see yourself as a sinners in need of salvation, there's not much even Jesus can do for you.

The reality for Jesus was that he would give all a chance to hear his gospel and receive his ministrations. But maybe, when it came to dining out, Jesus liked to enjoy himself rather than be carped at and criticized or stared at by people with condemnation in their eyes. So perhaps he gravitated more to the down-and-outers who appreciated him than the well-heeled and prosperous who didn't feel much need for him.

And isn't it the same today? Jesus probably wouldn't have been invited to the big society parties in New York and Washington DC, especially because he tended to speak his mind to such people and point out their sins. So it may be with us. We shouldn't, if we want to practice true faith in Christ, expect to make it as a socialite. The world will never love us unless they come to love our Savior.

75

Jesus ENTERED Jerusalem as Messiah and King.

What's the big deal about a guy riding into Jerusalem on a donkey? In Jesus's case, it was a very big deal. His actions made a bold statement: he was entering Israel's leading city as Messiah and king. The people immediately understood the implications—and welcomed them. The precedent of a newly crowned king entering his city riding on a donkey or mule was longstanding. When David wanted to show that Solomon was his anointed successor as king, he had Solomon ride on his own mule into the city amid a procession of people shouting praise to the new king (1 Kings 1:34–40).

In Jesus's day the Romans had made triumphal entries both common and spectacular. When a Roman general defeated some northern or southern tribe, he brought the prisoners back to Rome, where they became the centerpiece of long processions down the main boulevard of the city. Before the conquering army the people would walk, waving the branches of trees and ribbons, making a colorful entrance into the city. Then came the general and the army. Finally, walking in chains, if not dragged, were the vanquished thousands whose lot was to be sold in the markets to the highest bidders. In those days Rome's conquests never ceased, so the spectacles never ceased, and Rome always looked forward to such entries.

It has been said that a conquering king entered the city on a war-horse, while a king who came in peace entered on a gentle, lowly donkey. So on 9 Nisan AD 30, now known as Palm Sunday, when Jesus rode into Jerusalem as king, fulfilling prophecy, he rode on a humble donkey to symbolize his mission of peace. To march through the city in a chariot or with an army would never have suited him. He didn't come to take back his kingdom by force.

One interesting detail is that Jesus chose to ride on the back of a young colt that had never been ridden. That an unbroken animal could be ridden at all—much less in the chaos of a large, boisterous crowd pressing in on it—is itself a testament to Jesus's authority and power even over nature.

The people met Jesus coming from Bethphage, a small city on the edge of the Mount of Olives, just outside Jerusalem. They greeted him by laying their outer garments in the street and waving palm braches. Jesus rode on the "foal of a donkey," fulfilling a prophecy from Zechariah 9:9, which Matthew quoted to confirm its messianic application to Jesus: "Say to the Daughter of Zion, 'See, your king comes to you, gentle and riding on a donkey, on a colt, the foal of a donkey'" (Matthew 21:5).

The people of Jerusalem would have recognized immediately that this act related to Zechariah's prophecy, and they responded appropriately by crying out, "Hosanna [which means, "save now"] to the Son of David!" (Matthew 21:9). By using the title "Son of David," the people were recognizing Jesus as their legitimate king.

They quoted Psalm 118:26, "Blessed is he who comes in the name of the Lord!" and shouted their praise: "Hosanna in the highest."

This crowd, which may have included many Passover pilgrims from Galilee who were familiar with Jesus's ministry and miracles, welcomed Jesus as king and Messiah. Although they did not understand the full picture of what Jesus had come to accomplish, they were full of hope and ready to embrace him as the Son of David, the Messiah who would deliver them from Roman oppression. They didn't realize that through his death on the cross, he would reclaim all that was his, and Satan would be vanquished forever. That was the triumph of the "triumphal entry."

76

Jesus was the most popular man in Israel—and the most HATED.

Jesus seemed to be the most popular man in Israel. Wherever he went, crowds mobbed him. At one point the crowds wanted to make him king by force (see John 6:15). In a triumphal procession they welcomed him to Jerusalem as the Messiah, the Son of David. But even at the triumphal entry, there was another side to Jesus's popularity—a darker side. Everything that made Jesus beloved by one crowd made him feared and hated by another.

As the adoring crowd shouted, "Hosanna," the disenchanted Pharisees stewed and fumed all the more. "Teacher, rebuke your disciples!" they warned, indignant—or maybe alarmed (Luke 19:39). These Pharisees clearly rejected not only what the crowd was saying but also their effusiveness. They didn't like all this praise and adulation, and they certainly didn't believe Jesus was the coming king.

To this rebuke Jesus said, "If they keep quiet, the stones will cry out" (Luke 19:40). Then, as Jesus approached Jerusalem, he wept. "If you, even you, had only known on this day what would bring you peace—but now it is hidden from your eyes. The days will come upon you when your enemies will build an embankment against you and encircle you and hem you in on every side. They will dash you to the ground, you and the children within your walls. They will not leave one stone on another, because you did not recognize the time of God's coming to you" (Luke 19:42–44).

Note several things from this passage. Jesus wept. Something was wrong. He had just made his climactic entry into Jerusalem, where crowds hailed him as the coming king, but only Jesus saw the complete picture. They had hailed him as their king but not as their God and Savior. They were hoping for the inauguration of the messianic kingdom, a kingdom of peace that would last a thousand years (see Revelation 20:4). But Jesus saw coming destruction and misery, torture and pain—which happened in AD 70, when Rome's emperor Titus and his armies crushed the land of Israel, destroying the temple and prompting the Jews to disperse throughout the world.

The welcoming throng anticipated a political deliverer, a king and a kingdom. But Jesus came bringng a kingdom that was not of this world (see John 18:36), a spiritual rather than an earthly kingdom. He knew that the millennial kingdom was still in the distant future and that the near future would bring destruction, suffering, and sorrow. The irony was that the people of Jerusalem would be the cause of their own disappointment and suffering. Jesus clearly stated the reason for this coming destruction: "They will not leave one stone on another, because you did not recognize the time of God's coming to you" (Luke 19:44).

And the next week would tell the story. Jesus would purge the temple of the merchants and moneychangers, igniting the ire of the religious leaders who profited from those ventures. Then he would have repeated confrontations with the Pharisees, Sadducees, and Herodians.

In Matthew 27:15–26 we find another crowd; perhaps some were the same people who had welcomed Jesus on Palm Sunday. But this crowd was crying out something different: "Crucify him!" Though Jesus had been welcomed as a hero just five days earlier, now he was viciously condemned by another crowd of his fellow citizens. Finally, he would be tortured and executed.

How fickle the rule of the mob and the desire of the crowd. (Remember this when you read political poll statistics—or when you find the crowd singing your praises one day.)

Jesus gave Judas every POSSIBLE chance.

Judas Iscariot has, through the ages, been characterized as the worst sort of traitor. He went to the governing Jews and asked them what they would pay him to betray Jesus. They gave him thirty pieces of silver. It looked to everyone concerned that this was all about money.

In more recent times, through such plays as *Jesus Christ Superstar* and novels about Judas, it has been suggested that perhaps Judas didn't betray Jesus but rather was trying to get Jesus to act and usher in the messianic kingdom.

We don't really know Judas's motivation except that after turning against Jesus, he felt such remorse that he tried unsuccessfully to undo the deal and then went out and hanged himself (see Matthew 27:3–5).

But how did Jesus feel about Judas? Some insight comes from the Savior's last conversation with Judas, in the upper room where the disciples ate the last supper with Jesus. At some point during the dinner, Jesus said to the gathering, "I tell you the truth, one of you will betray me" (Matthew 26:20–21). The disciples, sad and afraid, each asked if he was the one. Jesus replied, "The one who has dipped his hand into the bowl with me will betray me. The Son of Man will go just as it is written about him. But woe to that man who betrays the Son of Man. If would be better for him if he had not been born" (Matthew 26:23–24).

Jesus specifically mentioned the sharing of bread. In Middle Eastern cultures the sharing of bread implied friendship and trust. To betray a person with whom you were close enough to share bread was particularly despicable.

The sharing of bread also fulfilled Scripture regarding the Messiah: "Even my close friend, whom I trusted, he who shared my bread, has lifted up his heel against me" (Psalm 41:9). Jesus himself quoted this verse at the Last Supper (see John 13:18).

John gives us an interesting take on the exchange between the disciples and Jesus. When asked who would betray him, Jesus answered, "'It is the one to whom I will give this piece of bread when I have dipped it in the dish.' Then, dipping the piece of bread, he gave it to Judas Iscariot, son of Simon" (John 13:26). This seems to indicate that Judas was sitting close to Jesus, perhaps even in the seat of honor.

After accepting the bread, Judas asked, "Surely not I, Rabbi?"

Jesus said directly to him, "Yes, it is you" (Matthew 26:25).

I believe that even as Judas had made his pact with the Pharisees and Sadducees and been paid the thirty pieces of silver; even as he planned to betray Jesus with a kiss; and even as he ate with the disciples, knowing what he was about to do, Jesus tried to bring him back. Jesus was warning Judas that he knew his plan and was giving him opportunities to change his intentions. Jesus gave Judas every chance to come back, even at the last moment.

But Judas didn't take that opportunity.

The truth remains, though, that Jesus tried. I believe that had Judas repented even at that point, Jesus would have embraced him and forgiven the whole thing. That Judas couldn't bring himself to do that says much about the darkness in his heart. At the same time, it's reassuring to us: we can know that even to the end, up until the last moment of our lives, Jesus reaches out, opens his arms, and asks for our faith and acceptance.

78

Jesus knew his FRIENDS would deny and abandon him.

Imagine facing the most difficult, harrowing trial of your life. Now imagine one of your closest friends bringing that trouble upon you, another friend denying you, and all the rest abandoning you to face it on your own. How would you cope with overwhelming difficulties with your support system missing—and with the added burden of knowing how badly your "friends" had failed you?

That's the situation Jesus was facing. But it didn't blindside him. It didn't even surprise him a little, although it's hard to believe it didn't make his heart ache. The gospel of John makes it clear that Jesus knew from the beginning how his end would come and that one of the Twelve he had chosen would betray him. Jesus had a special understanding of the human heart and of unique individuals. Even when the crowds believed his miracles and expressed faith in him, John says, "Jesus would not entrust himself to them, for he knew all men. He did not need man's testimony about man, for he knew what was in a man" (John 2:24–25).

Later in his ministry, after many disciples rejected Jesus's difficult sayings and deserted him, Peter led the way in pledging allegiance to Jesus. The Twelve vowed to remain faithful to Jesus to the end. But Jesus knew better. He told them, "Have I not chosen you, the Twelve? Yet one of you is a devil!" (He meant Judas, the son of Simon Iscariot, who, though one of the Twelve, was later to betray him) (John 6:70–71).

Again John noted Jesus's foreknowledge of his betrayal when he recorded the Lord's washing the disciples' feet: "Jesus knew that the time had come for him to leave this world and go to the Father" (John 13:1). When Jesus pronounced the disciples clean, he qualified it: "You are clean, though not every one of you" (John 13:10). Why did he say this? John says it's because "he knew who was going to betray him, and that was why he said not everyone was clean" (John 13:11).

At the Last Supper Jesus made it even more obvious and pointed out that he knew Judas would betray him: "I tell you the truth, one of you will betray me" (Matthew 26:21). When the grieved disciples asked one by one, "Surely not I?" Jesus told Judas pointedly, "Yes, it is you" (Matthew 26:25).

So Jesus knew Judas would betray him. But he also knew the others would fail him too. He knew that none of them would have the courage or strength to stand beside him in his time of trial. "You will all fall away," Jesus told them, "for it is written: 'I will strike the shepherd, and the sheep will be scattered.' But after I have risen, I will go ahead of you into Galilee" (Mark 14:26–28).

Peter—impetuous, brave Peter—couldn't imagine any situation in which he would abandon his beloved Master. "Peter declared, 'Even if all fall away, I will not.' 'I tell you the truth,' Jesus answered, 'today— yes, tonight—before the rooster crows twice you yourself will disown me three times.' But Peter insisted emphatically, 'Even if I have to die with you, I will never disown you.' And all the others said the same" (Mark 14:29–31). Their intentions were good, but Jesus knew that good intentions would not be enough. As he told the sleeping disciples in the Garden of Gethsemane later, "The spirit is willing, but the body is weak" (Mark 14:38).

But notice the love and kindness with which Jesus still acted toward those who he knew were going to betray, disown, and abandon him: "Having loved his own who were in the world, he now showed them the full extent of his love" (John 13:1). The Master lovingly washed the dirty feet of the servants. Almighty God washed the soles of lowly sinners.

Jesus said, "When you have turned back, strengthen your brothers." In other words, "When you've repented and come to your senses, go back to your brothers and help them learn to face the same sort of trials with victory and success." Jesus clearly felt confident that Peter would come through the situation with faith intact and with an ability to comfort his fellow disciples.

And notice the grace he expressed to Peter and the others, that even though they failed him, Jesus would take them back. Their relationship would not be irretrievably broken. After telling the disciples they would scatter and abandon him, Jesus encouraged them: "But after I have risen, I will go ahead of you into Galilee" (Mark 14:28). "Hey, guys, I'll meet up with you later," he was basically telling them. "It'll be OK. I know you'll fail, but I forgive you, and I'll want you back."

Jesus knew his friends would betray, disown, and abandon him during his darkest hours. But Jesus still loved them and called them "friends."

He knows the same about us, about our doubts, our fears, our betrayals too, when we fail to share our faith with someone out of fear they might reject us, or when we fail to own up to our beliefs when others criticize Christianity, the church, or even Jesus in our presence. Even though such acts pierce his heart, he knows our frailty and is merciful.

Jesus REDEEMS even
our failures.

It's one of the saddest moments in Peter's history. But what really happened? We find the story in Matthew 26, Mark 14, and Luke 22. Jesus told Peter ahead of time:

> "Simon, Simon, Satan has asked to sift you as wheat. But I have prayed for you, Simon, that your faith may not fail. And when you have turned back, strengthen your brothers."
>
> But he replied, "Lord, I am ready to go with you to prison and to death."
>
> Jesus answered, "I tell you, Peter, before the rooster crows today, you will deny three times that you know me." (Luke 22:31–34)

These words to Peter came shortly after Jesus had warned the disciples in the upper room that one of them would betray him. Note that Jesus addressed Peter as Simon rather than by his new name. Jesus had done this at other times too, usually when Peter had flubbed up, as if to say, "You're going back to your Simon days, Peter. Buck up and act like Rocky (that's what "Peter" means in Greek), instead of like your old self."

What Jesus told Peter should give us all pause, for surely Satan seeks the same privilege of working us over as he did Peter. Jesus told Peter that Satan had desired to "sift him as wheat." What does that mean? When you sift wheat, you use a sieve or other instrument to separate the chaff from the kernels. Satan wanted to show God (and Jesus) that Peter was little more than chaff and that all the disciple's proud talk meant nothing. In other words, Satan wanted to test Peter's mettle and prove him a coward unworthy of God's love and confidence.

As if to add to the burden, Jesus said that he had prayed that Peter's faith would not fail. That is, though Peter might fall because of his lack of courage, he wouldn't give up believing in Jesus as his Lord and Master.

How did it all work out?

As the soldiers dragged Jesus away to his first trial before Annas, the former high priest, Peter stood outside in the courtyard by a fire, warming his hands. Various people said they recognized him as one of the disciples or, because of his Galilean accent, that he must be one of Jesus's followers. Peter became more and more emphatic as the questions went on, until he actually swore that he never knew Jesus.

When the cock crowed, Peter saw his villainy and hurried out to some lonely spot to weep his eyes out.

I believe Satan tries to launch this kind of attack on every believer, or at least those who are laboring successfully in the fields of spiritual harvest. Why? Notice what Jesus said to Peter: "Satan has asked to sift you as wheat." In Luke's account the text reads that Satan "has demanded permission" (Luke 22:31 NASB). Why would Satan need permission?

For an answer, let's go back to Job 1:8–11, where Satan sought to test another man of God:

> The LORD said to Satan, "Have you considered my servant Job? There is no one on earth like him; he is blameless and upright, a man who fears God and shuns evil."
>
> "Does Job fear God for nothing?" Satan replied. "Have you not put a hedge around him and his household and everything he has? You have blessed the work of his hands, so that his flocks and herds are spread throughout the land. But stretch out your hand and strike everything he has, and he will surely curse you to your face."

This exchange between Satan and God points out a great truth: God had put a hedge around Job as one of his children. God has put the same hedge around each of his children throughout the world. Satan can't break through and touch any of us unless God gives him permission. And God only gives permission when he knows the time is right.

That's a tremendous promise: Satan can't touch any of us unless God says so. And after we have been tested, we, too, should strengthen our brothers and sisters in Christ.

80

Jesus heard VOICES from heaven.

Jesus had two things in common with people we put in padded cells: he said he was God, and he heard voices from heaven. But Jesus wasn't insane: he truly is God—the voices from heaven said so.

At Jesus's baptism, God spoke from heaven in a loud voice, saying, "This is my Son, whom I love; with him I am well pleased" (Matthew 3:17). But that was just the first time. The Gospels record two additional incidents when God spoke aloud to Jesus and the people present.

In Matthew 17:1–8 Jesus took three disciples—Peter, James, and John, the "inner circle" of the Twelve—up on a mountain to pray. There Jesus was transfigured—his clothing became as white as the light, and his face shone like the sun. "Just then there appeared before them Moses and Elijah, talking with Jesus" (Matthew 17:3). After Jesus had conferred for a while with these great prophets and leaders from Israel's past, God spoke from heaven a second time. He said, "This is my Son, whom I love; with him I am well pleased. Listen to him!" (Matthew 17:5). These words are almost identical to the words spoken at Jesus's baptism: only the admonition, "Listen to him!" is added.

The third time a voice spoke from heaven is recorded in John 12:20–36. Jesus said that his hour to be glorified had come, and he knew he would soon die. He concluded, "Now my heart is troubled, and what shall I say? 'Father, save me from this hour'? No, it was for this very reason I came to this hour. Father, glorify your name" (John 12:27–28).

As if on cue, God spoke. "I have glorified it, and will glorify it again" (John 12:28). Everyone heard something, but their judgment varied as to what it was and its significance. Some believed it must have been thunder; others concluded it must have been an angel speaking to Jesus. But Jesus knew exactly who it was—and why his Father had spoken.

Jesus said, "This voice was for your benefit, not mine. Now is the time for judgment on this world; now the prince of this world will be driven out. But I, when I am lifted up from the earth, will draw all men to myself" (John 12:30–31).

Jesus gave the purpose for all three heavenly messages: They were "for your benefit, not mine." It was God's way of giving his stamp of approval to Jesus's ministry, as if he signed off on the mission report and said, "Hey, everyone, check this guy out. He's the person to watch! Jesus is God!" The voices said so.

81

Jesus SANG.

The Bible is full of music. Much worship in the temple happened through music. David was a harpist and composed more than eighty songs that are now found in the book of Psalms (which means "songs"). Orchestras, instruments, all we might think of as part of contemporary worship were available in ancient times. The Jews were known far and wide for their beautiful music. Psalm 137:1–3 says, "By the rivers of Babylon we sat and wept when we remembered Zion. There on the poplars we hung our harps, for there our captors asked us for songs, our tormentors demanded songs of joy; they said, 'Sing us one of the songs of Zion!'"

Even some of Paul's writings include passages some scholars believe could have been psalms, praise songs, or recitations (see Ephesians 5:14; 1 Timothy 3:16; and 2 Timothy 2:11–13). Paul said twice that when the Spirit fills us, we speak to one another in "psalms, hymns, and spiritual songs" (see Ephesians 5:19; Colossians 3:16). So it just makes sense that any respectable Jew might be excused if, at any moment, he might suddenly belt out one of the famous songs of Zion.

With such a musical tradition long established in the worship and life of Israel, it's worth asking, did Jesus ever sing?

Tucked into a little transition verse in the book of Mark, we read these words about Jesus and his disciples at the Last Supper: "When they had sung a hymn, they went out to the Mount of Olives" (Mark 14:26). We don't know if Jesus was a tenor, bass, or baritone. We aren't told if Bartholomew, Philip, and James broke out into three-part harmony. We have no idea what the hymn was or how long it lasted. But they sang it, and I wonder if the words didn't catch in Jesus's throat as he realized that those would be his last truly joyous moments with his disciples while on earth in his first incarnation.

82

Jesus probably DANCED.

The Old Testament talks about dancing in many places, but the New Testament rarely mentions it. Still, dancing is a strong Jewish tradition, and wedding feasts would have featured some dancing, although probably only women with women and men with men.

The one time Jesus did refer to dancing in a way that makes one think it was a common activity for Jews, he did it indirectly. In Luke 7:33 he spoke about John the Baptist. He had come with fasting, baptism, and repentance, all rather somber activities. Jesus's ministry brought an outpouring of grace—uplifting words, astonishing miracles, and a Savior come to redeem mankind. But many of the Jews weren't satisfied by either. That's why Jesus said, "To what, then, can I compare the people of this generation? What are they like? They are like children sitting in the marketplace and calling out to each other: 'We played the flute for you, and you did not dance; we sang a dirge, and you did not cry'" (Luke 7:31–32).

So, did Jesus ever dance? Surely, in attending all those weddings and other gatherings, there were moments when people pulled out their instruments, struck up the band, and danced. Did Jesus join them? The Bible doesn't say, but it does offer a clue. Several psalms mention dancing, most notably Psalm 150. Jewish worship included dancing as a way to worship God. King David and the people of Israel "were celebrating with all their might before the LORD" (2 Samuel 6:5) as the Ark of the Covenant was being brought back to Jerusalem. Many translations, including the King James Version, translate "celebrating" as "dancing."

When Jesus worshiped his Father, should we think the only thing he did was bow and pray? Were there not moments of exuberant joy and enthusiastic celebration?

John 21:25 says, "Jesus did many other things as well. If every one of them were written down, I suppose that even the whole world would not have room for the books that would be written."

And we do know from another text that Jesus sang: shortly before Jesus's arrest in the Garden of Gethsemane, he and his disciples sang a hymn (Mark 14:26). No one knows what hymn they sang—or what else they did. But it doesn't seem a stretch to believe that, like his ancestor David, Jesus knew enough joy in the Lord to celebrate and worship with dance.

83

Jesus was SOLD for the price of a slave.

When Judas Iscariot decided to betray Jesus, he went to the priests and made a deal. They gave him thirty pieces of silver to do this.

Why thirty pieces of silver?

Scripture gives us two reasons. One comes from Exodus 21:32, which set the price of compensation for a slave gored by an ox. The owner of the ox was to pay the slave's owner thirty pieces of silver—the value of a gored slave in those days. Thus, the priests were willing to pay for Jesus the same sum they'd pay for a dead slave.

The second reason is found in Zechariah 11. This prophecy takes the form of a story about a shepherd who fails to protect or love his flock of sheep. The shepherd asked for payment, and Zechariah says, "They paid me thirty pieces of silver" (Zechariah 11:12). Once again, this seems to indicate the standard price for a slave.

Zechariah's writing points inexorably to Jesus, not only for the price paid for his betrayal, but also for what became of the blood money: "'Throw it to the potter'—the handsome price at which they priced me! So I took the thirty pieces of silver and threw them into the house of the LORD to the potter" (Zechariah 11:13). This was fulfilled when Judas, seized with remorse, returned the thirty silver coins to the chief priests and the elders. "'I have sinned,' he said, 'for I have betrayed innocent blood.' 'What is that to us?' they replied. 'That's your responsibility.' So Judas threw the money into the temple and left. Then he went away and hanged himself. The chief priests picked up the coins and said, 'It is against the law to put this into the treasury, since it is blood money.' So they decided to use the money to buy the potter's field as a burial place for foreigners. That is why it has been called the Field of Blood to this day" (Matthew 27:3–8).

What is the point of this story? The Jews of Jesus's day valued him no more than if he had been a common slave.

84

Jesus DIDN'T want to suffer and die.

Did you ever do something you absolutely didn't want to do? Not when you were a little kid and your parents forced you—or as an adult when your boss, your spouse, or social pressure made you do something you dreaded. Have you ever done something that made you want to turn and run the other direction, but you did it anyway just because it was the right thing to do? If so, you'll understand a little better how Jesus must have felt about his impending death on the cross.

Matthew, Mark, and Luke record Jesus's emotional prayer as he grappled with his feelings about the very real, very horrible death he would face in just a matter of hours. Mark 14:32–42 is the most extensive, detailed passage. There we find that Jesus had taken three disciples—Peter, James, and John—into the Garden of Gethsemane, an olive grove on the Mount of Olives. Jesus often went there to pray (see John 18:2).

Jesus said to the three, "My soul is overwhelmed with sorrow to the point of death" (Mark 14:34). Today we know it's possible for a person to die because of inner anguish and grief, and what Jesus must have been feeling was so intense he likened it to the point of death.

After this he withdrew a short distance to pray. "He fell to the ground and prayed that if possible the hour might pass from him. 'Abba [the Aramaic word for "Daddy"], Father,' he said, 'everything is possible for you. Take this cup from me. Yet not what I will, but what you will'"(Mark 14:36).

Jesus then returned to the disciples and found them sleeping. He rebuked them and went back to his prayer, saying the same thing to his Father. This he did three times. The last time he returned to the disciples, he said, "Are you still sleeping and resting? Enough! The hour has come. Look, the Son of Man is betrayed into the hands of sinners. Rise! Let us go! Here comes my betrayer" (Mark 14:41–42).

Clearly Jesus asked that his Father release him from the responsibility of going to the cross. He asked this three times, a special number in the Bible that signifies perfection (God is a trinity—three in one). But if this prayer was his perfect request, his conclusion was even more perfect: "Yet not what I will, but what you will." Though Jesus in his spirit and humanity shrank from the task he had come to perform, he ultimately chose to obey his Father rather than his own desires. It was God's will for Jesus to go to the cross. So Jesus went.

He did it not because he had to but because it was the right thing to do.

85

Jesus was jerked around at his SO-CALLED trial.

In the United States we're accustomed to certain forms of justice. For instance, double jeopardy (being tried more than once for the same crime) is illegal in our country. Every person arrested has certain rights—Miranda and so on—that prevent authorities from taking advantage of the little guy. And if you can't afford a lawyer (at $250 an hour or more), the court will appoint one for you to work for free.

If you're convicted of a crime, you can appeal the court decision and ask for a new trial. If you still don't get satisfaction, you can take your case all the way to the Supreme Court, whose nine justices are steeped in the law and can spot the slightest infraction on the part of the authorities.

With this in mind, let's go back to the trials of Jesus. After his arrest on no explicit charges (an illegal thing to do), Jesus stood trial before Annas (see John 18:12–23), who had been out of office as high priest for fifteen years and had no real legal authority. Annas questioned Jesus about "his disciples and his teaching." This was another illegal move, for according to Jewish law witnesses were supposed to be brought in first to establish guilt. The weight of establishing guilt was on the authorities, not the weight of proving innocence on the accused. Jesus responded that he'd taught openly all over the country and that the priest should ask one of his listeners to confirm what he'd said. For such straightforwardness (or impudence, as the high priest took it), one of the officers struck Jesus in the face, another illegal action.

Unable to get Jesus to admit to wrongdoing or do something that could justifiably be called a crime, Annas sent Jesus to Caiaphas to stand trial before the Sanhedrin, the official high court of justice in ancient Jerusalem. In Matthew 26:57–68 we see the exchanges. They brought many false witnesses against Jesus, but none of their testimony held until Caiaphas charged Jesus under oath to tell them if he was the Christ, the Son of God. Legally obligated to respond, Jesus answered truthfully: "Yes, it is as you say" (Matthew 26:64). That admission sealed Jesus's fate before the Sanhedrin. As far as they were concerned, Jesus had committed the ultimate blasphemy by claiming to be God in the flesh.

Since the Sanhedrin, under Roman jurisdiction, couldn't sentence anyone to death, Caiaphas allowed his people to spit on Jesus, mock him, and hit him. But they needed the Romans to condemn Jesus, too, so he could be put to death. To this end Caiaphas sent Jesus on to his third trial before the Roman governor of Judea, Pontius Pilate. By now it was early morning.

The Jewish leaders took Jesus before Pilate with a series of trumped up charges calculated to make Jesus look bad to Roman sensibilities: "We have found this man subverting our nation. He opposes payment of taxes to Caesar and claims to be Christ, a king. . . . He stirs up the people all over Judea by his teaching" (Luke 23:2, 5). Pilate quickly realized Jesus was innocent. He said so multiple times to the crowd, but they kept insisting that Jesus should be put to death. Matthew 27:18 indicates that Pilate "knew it was out of envy that they had handed Jesus over to him." Even Pilate's uninvolved wife knew Jesus was innocent. She warned Pilate: "Don't have anything to do with that innocent man, for I have suffered a great deal today in a dream because of him" (Matthew 27:19).

Pilate tried to weasel out of the deliberations, and when he learned Jesus was a Galilean, he thought he'd found his way out. Herod, Pilate's rival, had jurisdiction over Galilee. It would suit Pilate just fine to wash his hands of this troubling case and let Herod make the call, so he sent Jesus on to Herod for a fourth trial. There, according to Luke 23:8–12,

Herod was anxious to see Jesus. He hoped he might see Jesus perform some miracle. Herod interrogated Jesus at length, but Jesus wouldn't say a word and certainly wouldn't perform divine tricks. Herod then handed Jesus over to his soldiers, who mocked him, placed a robe over his shoulders, and sarcastically hailed him as king. Then Herod returned Jesus to Pilate without a conviction.

Upon his return to Pilate—his fifth trial—Pilate made this pronouncement to the throng thirsty for Jesus's blood: "You brought me this man as one who was inciting the people to rebellion. I have examined him in your presence and have found no basis for your charges against him. Neither has Herod, for he sent him back to us; as you can see, he has done nothing to deserve death" (Luke 23:14–15). So far so good. But then Pilate added a compromise he thought would satisfy their bloodlust: he would punish Jesus, even though he was innocent, and then release him. He would turn Jesus over to the soldiers for scourging. This involved being beaten mercilessly with a whip (probably a cat o' nine tails) that tore the flesh from his back and legs and reduced a person to little more than a bloody heap.

But this was not sufficient for Jesus's accusers. They threatened Pilate: "If you let this man go, you are no friend of Caesar. Anyone who claims to be a king opposes Caesar" (John 19:12). That did it for Pilate's flagging resolve. He didn't want his loyalty to Caesar questioned, so he condemned Jesus to death. But Pilate still thought he had one more trick up his sleeve to free the innocent man who just might be a king and the Son of God. It was the custom at Passover to free a Jewish prisoner sentenced to death, and Pilate proposed that Jesus be that man. But the crowd, stirred up by the leading Jews, shrieked for Jesus's crucifixion. Pilate, probably fearing a riot and losing complete control of the situation, gave in to their pressure. He sentenced Jesus to death.

Jesus suffered through many breaches of justice in his multiple trials. Not a shred of justice was produced at any of them to show he had committed any crime or should have been sentenced to death. Imagine angels standing by with swords drawn, who could have struck down the mob and saved Jesus. Imagine the Father himself looking on. Although he knew the end from the beginning and the purpose of Jesus's death, it still must have broken his heart.

Jesus was innocent. Pilate could find no fault in him. The Jews believed he'd committed blasphemy, but all he'd done was tell them the truth he'd been repeating to his disciples and followers: in essence, "Believe in me, and I will give you eternal life."

It would have been so simple for some sane person to cry out, "What is this madness? This man has done nothing wrong, and judging from his life and mission, he might really be God incarnate. How can we do this to the person who might be our Messiah?"

But if that was shouted out by a few believers, their voices were never given an honest hearing. The reality is, when God came down to show us how to live, the people who said they wanted him the most tore him to pieces.

86

Jesus was judged NOT guilty . . . and executed anyway.

Philosopher Friedrich Nietzsche claimed that Jesus was executed for his political guilt, because he was basically a rebel. But when we look at the record, we find this isn't true.

Pilate repeatedly argued that he could not find Jesus guilty of any offense. After Jesus first appeared before Pilate, the Roman returned his verdict to the Jews: "I find no basis for a charge against him" (John 18:38).

Learning that Jesus was a Galilean, Pilate tried to foist the case on Herod, who had jurisdiction in that region. But when Herod tired of the game and sent Jesus back to Pilate, Pilate was forced to grapple with the issue again. He announced to Jesus's enemies: "I have examined him in your presence and have found no basis for your charges against him. Neither has Herod, for he sent him back to us; as you can see, he has done nothing to deserve death. Therefore I will punish him and then release him" (Luke 23:14–16).

He sent Jesus to the Roman praetorium, where they whipped him, dressed him in a fine robe, pressed a crown of thorns on his head, and mocked him. Perhaps Pilate thought this would satisfy the bloodthirsty mob, so he brought Jesus out wearing the crown of thorns and the robe and said, "Look, I am bringing him out to you to let you know that I find no basis for a charge against him" (John 19:4).

But it wasn't enough for the chief priests and religious leaders. They cried out, "Crucify! Crucify!" (John 19:6). Knowing that the Jewish leaders had handed Jesus over to him out of envy (see Mark 15:10), Pilate tried yet again to spare Jesus: he tried swapping the life of Jesus for that of a violent, notorious criminal, Barabbas. It was a custom for Pilate to release one prisoner to please the people at the time of the Passover feast. But the Jews demanded that Pilate release Barabbas, an insurrectionist and murderer, rather than the innocent Jesus. So Pilate told them, "You take him and crucify him. As for me, I find no basis for a charge against him" (John 19:6). But Pilate and the Jewish leaders both knew that under Roman rule, they had no power or authority to execute anyone. For that, they needed Pilate.

The leaders responded, "We have a law, and according to that law he must die, because he claimed to be the Son of God" (John 19:7).

This instilled even more fear in Pilate. He walked back to Jesus and questioned him further. When Jesus refused to answer, neither begged nor pleaded for his life, Pilate said in frustration, "Don't you realize I have power either to free you or to crucify you?" (John 19:10). But Jesus replied, "You would have no power over me if it were not given to you from above" (John 19:11).

The account in John 19:12–16 continues:

> From then on, Pilate tried to set Jesus free, but the Jews kept shouting, "If you let this man go, you are no friend of Caesar. Anyone who claims to be a king opposes Caesar."
>
> When Pilate heard this, he brought Jesus out and sat down on the judge's seat at a place known as the Stone Pavement (which in Aramaic is Gabbatha). It was the day of Preparation of Passover Week, about the sixth hour.
>
> "Here is your king," Pilate said to the Jews.
>
> But they shouted, "Take him away! Take him away! Crucify him!"
>
> "Shall I crucify your king?" Pilate asked.

"We have no king but Caesar," the chief priests answered.
Finally Pilate handed him over to them to be crucified

From this we can note that Pilate seriously tried to release Jesus. That does not absolve him of guilt: he capitulated to mob rule. But clearly, he saw that Jesus had violated no Roman law. Jesus was crucified at the insistence of the some of the leading Jews because he claimed to be the Son of God, God incarnate, the Messiah. If Jesus was not the Son of God, God incarnate, Messiah, then they crucified him justly.

As it was, they murdered more than an innocent man: they executed the Son of God, God incarnate, the Messiah.

87

Jesus's blood is on all OUR hands.

One very interesting statement, found only in the book of Matthew, concerns who took responsibility for the death of Jesus. The Romans? The Jews? God? Others?

It wasn't the Romans, because Pilate found no guilt in Jesus and actually wanted to set him free. He only did the will of the crowd for fear of a riot.

Although God had planned Jesus's death and resurrection from before the foundation of the world, he did not carry out the sentence himself, in some physical or supernatural sense. Isaiah says, "It was the LORD's will to crush him and cause him to suffer, and though the LORD makes his life a guilt offering, he will see his offspring and prolong his days" (Isaiah 53:10). But even though it was "the Lord's will" to send Jesus to the cross, God was not to blame for Jesus's death.

Some of the Jewish leaders seemed willing to accept responsibility at the time. At Jesus's trial, when the Roman governor Pilate tried to free Jesus, they insisted he be crucified, saying, "Let his blood be on us and on our children" (Matthew 27:25). Though some people use that to pin responsibility for Jesus's death on the Jewish people, those who had clamored for his crucifixion were in fact a very small segment of the Hebrew people—the Sadducees and Pharisees who most hated Jesus. Many more Jews actually supported him.

Not even the beating Jesus received before his execution, the blood he lost while on the cross, or the brutality of the crucifixion itself are what actually killed him. It would take something much greater to send him into the realm of death.

What was it?

Sin. In that moment, as Jesus bore the penalty for the sins of every person who had ever lived, was living at the time, or would live, he took on a burden that literally destroyed him spiritually, emotionally, and physically.

So who killed him?

You, me, and every last one of us.

88

Jesus FULFILLED precise details of prophecy as he died.

Many passages in the Old Testament have been pointed out as prophecies of Jesus's death on the cross. Many are individual verses that seem thrown into the text out of nowhere. However, one primary passage, Psalm 22, records a number of elements of the crucifixion that are remarkable for their accuracy and straightforwardness. David wrote this psalm more than eight hundred years before the death of Christ, and probably six or seven hundred years before crucifixion was used by the Romans as their primary form of execution.

Let's consider a few of the prophetic statements:

Verse 1: "My God, my God, why have you forsaken me?" This was Jesus's fifth statement from the cross, a cry from an abject sense of abandonment and desolation as he bore the sins of the world.

Verses 6–7: "I am a worm and not a man, scorned by men and despised by the people. All who see me mock me; they hurl insults, shaking their heads." This perfectly reflects the scorn and mocking of the crowd as Jesus hung on the cross. Nothing in David's life, no event, no situation, mirrors this. It's pure prophecy.

Verse 8: "He trusts in the LORD; let the LORD rescue him." This is almost exactly what the mockers told Jesus on the cross: "He saved others," they said, "but he can't save himself! . . . He trusts in God. Let

God rescue him now if he wants him" (Matthew 27:42–43). These words from the mouths of those who didn't believe Jesus was the Messiah not only echo prophecy but are its fulfillment.

Verse 11: "Do not be far from me, for trouble is near and there is no one to help." Jesus hung on the cross utterly alone. This echoes the cry of verse 1.

Verses 12–13: "Many bulls surround me; strong bulls of Bashan encircle me. Roaring lions tearing their prey open their mouths wide against me." This is an image of the many powerful enemies who surrounded Jesus on that fateful day.

Verse 14: "I am poured out like water, and all my bones are out of joint." Crucifixion caused tremendous thirst (Jesus thirsted on the cross and said so—see John 19:28) and also puts the shoulder, thigh, and foot bones out of joint. It makes one feel as though his own body has completely betrayed him.

Verse 14: "My heart has turned to wax; it has melted away within me." Imagine how difficult it would be to remain courageous in the face of such an onslaught.

Verse 15: "My strength is dried up like a potsherd, and my tongue sticks to the roof of my mouth; you lay me in the dust of death." With the loss of fluids from the flogging and crucifixion, Christ would have suffered from deep loss of strength and dry mouth.

Verse 16: "Dogs have surrounded me; a band of evil men has encircled me, they have pierced my hands and my feet." The word *dogs* was commonly used of Gentiles, which the Roman soldiers were; "evil men" referred to the oppressing Jews. And one can get no more definitive description of crucifixion than the last line—"they have pierced my hands and my feet."

Verse 18: "They divide my garments among them and cast lots for my clothing." In John 19:23–24 we see that this is exactly what happened. The Roman soldiers crucifying Jesus divided his clothes among them. Recognizing the value of Christ's cloak, a seamless garment, they decided to cast lots for his clothing because they didn't want to tear it up. To the winner went the spoils. John specifically quotes Psalm 22:18 and cites the soldiers' actions as fulfilling this prophecy.

From the words in Psalm 22 we see a perfect description of the conditions of crucifixion as well as the scene that surrounded Jesus at the time and the events that had overtaken him. Down to the strangest details, we see history unfolding according to God's plan in David's psalm and in the crucifixion.

If a Jew had referred to Psalm 22 at the time, which was considered a messianic psalm—one that predicted the life and times of the Messiah—he would have recognized the uncanny parallel. Only someone who knew the future could have composed those prophetic lines. It wasn't David but the Spirit who inspired this psalm.

89

Jesus's REASON for living was to die.

Some people think that Jesus's crucifixion cut short the promising life of a good teacher. Others go so far as to believe that the life of an exceptional prophet—dare we even say the Son of God—was derailed by a tragic, horrible mistake. If only God had been able to protect him. If only Jesus had gone to Beersheba instead of Jerusalem that weekend. If only . . .

But such people are selling Jesus short—*way* short. Jesus made clear that the whole reason he had come into the world was to die for the sins of the world. Question: if Jesus had lived a great life, taught many wonderful things, done miracles to the point of eliminating disease from humanity, and lived long and healthy until making a happy departure, would he have fulfilled his purpose?

No. Jesus's whole purpose was to die. This was the plan announced from the start of Jesus's life. When Jesus was just a few days old, Simeon, a prophet who awaited the coming of the Messiah, said to Mary, "This child is destined to cause the falling and rising of many in Israel, and to be a sign that will be spoken against, so that the thoughts of many hearts will be revealed. And a sword will pierce your own soul too" (Luke 2:34–35). What could that sword have been in Mary's heart but the crucifixion?

Repeatedly Jesus forewarned his disciples that he would be arrested, mocked, killed, and then would rise again (see Matthew 16:21; 17:22–23; 20:17–19). Early on, with increasing clarity and forcefulness, Jesus began preparing the disciples for the great event of his ministry—his death on the cross.

In John 10:17–18 we find Jesus telling a group listening to him in the temple, "The reason my Father loves me is that I lay down my life—only to take it up again. No one takes it from me, but I lay it down of my own accord. I have authority to lay it down, and I have authority to take it up again." In this instance Jesus was telling many people, not just his immediate circle of disciples, that he planned to die and rise again.

Jesus even told his enemies. When the Pharisees and teachers of the Law demanded a miracle to prove Jesus's authority, Jesus responded: "A wicked and adulterous generation asks for a miraculous sign! But none will be given it except the sign of the prophet Jonah. For as Jonah was three days and three nights in the belly of a huge fish, so the Son of Man will be three days and three nights in the heart of the earth" (Matthew 12:39–40). Again, Jesus told them, "Destroy this temple, and I will raise it again in three days" (John 2:19). They knew what Jesus meant by these statements, too, for after he died they asked Pilate for permission to post a guard at his tomb. "We remember that while he was still alive that deceiver said, 'After three days I will rise again.' So give the order for the tomb to be made secure until the third day. Otherwise, his disciples may come and steal the body and tell the people that he has been raised from the dead" (Matthew 27:63–64).

Later, when Jesus went back to Jerusalem after being gone for some time, he talked about how a seed must be put into the ground and then die to produce fruit. Then he added, rather cryptically, "Now my heart is troubled, and what shall I say? 'Father, save me from this hour'? No, it was for this very reason I came to this hour" (John 12:27). He was clearly referring to his death, reinforcing the truth that the whole reason he had come to earth in the flesh was for the hour of his sacrifice.

At Jesus's arrest Peter cut off the ear of the priest's servant with a sword. But Jesus rebuked him and reaffirmed his commitment to fulfill his mission. He said to all present—soldiers, leaders of the Jews, and

Jesus's own disciples—"Do you think I cannot call on my Father, and he will at once put at my disposal more than twelve legions of angels? But how then would the Scriptures be fulfilled that say it must happen in this way?" (Matthew 26:53–54). If Jesus had wanted to be rescued, he had his chance and said so. The Father would have sent seventy-two thousand angels to help him (twelve legions, six thousand soldiers per legion). But Jesus knew the Scriptures had to be fulfilled: he had to die.

Jesus clearly saw his arrest and subsequent death as part and parcel of his whole reason for being. When Pontius Pilate became angry because Jesus would not answer his questions, he said, "Don't you realize I have power either to free you or to crucify you?" (John 19:10). Jesus answered, "You would have no power over me if it were not given you from above" (John 19:11).

Even here Jesus saw that events were not being guided by human beings but by God, as Acts 2:23 says: "This man was handed over to you by God's set purpose and foreknowledge; and you, with the help of wicked men, put him to death by nailing him to the cross."

Jesus saw his whole life as moving inexorably toward the moment of crisis on the cross. He could have avoided it; he could have had the help of legions of angels if he wanted to escape. But Jesus submitted to what he was destined for and went to the cross without flinching.

90

Jesus gave eternal life to the THIEF on the cross.

"Deathbed conversions." Hear of them? "Foxhole believers." Know about those?

Over the years I've heard of many people who have waited until the end of their lives to make that all-important statement of faith. Some downplay such conversions, saying that many probably aren't real. Dr. James Dobson reported that Ted Bundy, the serial murderer, made a "profession of faith" shortly before he was executed. Jeffrey Dahmer, the "cannibal murderer" who ate parts of the bodies of his victims, also supposedly confessed Christ while in prison, sometime before he was murdered there.

Whether such people actually made it to heaven, we don't know. However, one case in the Gospels proves that at least some such conversions are very real. We know one dying man found his heavenly destination through Jesus, because Jesus said so. This man was one of the two thieves crucified with Jesus. We don't know his name or even his crime. Luke 23:32–33 says, "Two other men, both criminals, were also led out with him to be executed. When they came to the place called the Skull, there they crucified him, along with the criminals—one on his right, the other on his left."

According to Matthew 27:44 and Mark 15:32, the criminals initially mocked Jesus. However, as time wore on—six hours on the cross for Jesus and probably longer for the thieves—one of the men had a change of heart. "One of the criminals who hung there hurled insults at him: 'Aren't you the Christ? Save yourself and us!' But the other criminal rebuked him. 'Don't you fear God, since you are under the same sentence? We are punished justly, for we are getting what our deeds deserve. But this man has done nothing wrong.' Then he said, 'Jesus, remember me when you come into your kingdom'" (Luke 23:39–42).

Jesus must have been listening the whole time, even with the rest of the crowd hurling abuse at him. He said to this repentant criminal, "I tell you the truth, today you will be with me in paradise" (Luke 23:43).

Was the thief sincere? Did he make a real profession of faith? I suspect when you're dying on a cross, you can't get much more sincere as you think about where you're headed. This man had a real change of heart. For one thing, he recognized that Jesus was an innocent man, which means that he must also have understood that the Jews had sent him to the cross for blasphemy. If this man believed Jesus was innocent, then he must have believed Jesus was the Messiah.

He also admitted his guilt, a key element in any profession of faith.

And he spoke of fearing God, something perhaps brought home by the teachings of his youth or at other times.

Next he spoke of Jesus coming into a kingdom, a recognition of Jesus's kingship and the fact that he did indeed have a kingdom he would rule.

Finally, he threw himself on the mercy of Jesus with the words, "Remember me when . . . " He had nothing to offer Christ, no grand list of deeds or works others might bring to Jesus in such a situation. Rather, he asked for mercy and grace, the ultimate right thing to do when we ask God for anything.

Jesus affirmed this man's faith and gave him a grand promise, which resonates through the ages to all who might find themselves facing death. Jesus will not turn away any who cry out for mercy from God. As Jesus said in John 6:37, "All that the Father gives me will come to me, and whoever comes to me I will never drive away."

91

As he was dying, Jesus FORGAVE those who were killing him.

Forgetting the father's kindness to them, they killed his beloved son. As he was dying, the son said, "May the Lord see this and call you to account." That was the prophet Zechariah, son of the priest Jehoiada (2 Chronicles 24:22). Were you thinking of Jesus? No. Jesus was the guy who, while he was dying a horribly agonizing death on the cross, said something truly remarkable: "Father, forgive them, for they do not know what they are doing" (Luke 23:34).

Who was Jesus talking about? Was he speaking only of the Roman soldiers who had done the dirty work as ordered, nailing Jesus to the cross and erecting it between two thieves? Or did Jesus's extravagant forgiveness extend to others?

Jesus's forgiveness knew no limits. He was forgiving all his tormentors—the Romans, and those who mocked him as he hung there, the religious leaders who had pursued and condemned him, and everyone else through the ages who had or would reject Christ without really understanding who he is. Jesus forgave them because they were ignorant: they didn't really know they were murdering God incarnate, the one who had come to take away their sins. In Acts 13:27 Paul, while explaining the gospel, said, "The people of Jerusalem and their rulers did not recognize Jesus, yet in condemning him they fulfilled the words of the prophets." First

Corinthians 2:8 also says, "None of the rulers of this age understood it, for if they had, they would not have crucified the Lord of glory."

Is Jesus's forgiveness offered because of ignorance? Absolutely. That doesn't mean the people deserved forgiveness or that it didn't come at a price. But Jesus extended to them a forgiveness based on their lack of understanding. If they had truly comprehended that he was the Son of God, they never would have crucified him.

But what about those who did know, who understood exactly who Jesus was? There weren't any, at least not among those who sent him to the cross. Some in the crowd who witnessed his crucifixion undoubtedly believed in Jesus, and although they might not have understood all the ramifications of what was happening, they put their trust in him and were redeemed.

In effect, Jesus's forgiveness covered all of them—those who were complicit in his murder because they didn't know he was the Son of God, and those who believed in him already.

92

Jesus WILLED his mother to a disciple.

Dying without a will is serious business today. The court takes the deceased person's estate and doles it out as it sees fit. A loved one's dying "intestate" is a grim problem for many families. But Jesus was ahead of the curve. Although wills may not have been the big business they are today, Jesus made clear what to do with his treasures before he died. How and when did Jesus record his last will and testament? He gave it from the cross. What did Jesus have that was worth carefully entrusting to the person of his choice? Jesus had one treasure of value to give, and he gave it. What was it? His mother, Mary.

In John 19:25–27, we read: "Near the cross of Jesus stood his mother, his mother's sister, Mary the wife of Clopas, and Mary Magdalene. When Jesus saw his mother there, and the disciple whom he loved standing nearby, he said to his mother, 'Dear woman, here is your son,' and to the disciple, 'Here is your mother.' From that time on, this disciple took her into his home."

We don't know the status of Jesus's family at the time of the cross, but we do know Jesus was Mary's eldest son. It was the eldest son's responsibility to take care of the parents when they were old. Since Jesus was dying and would soon go to heaven, he wanted to make sure his mother (his father, Joseph, had likely died earlier) would be cared for. Thus, he gave this charge to John, his disciple, one of the inner three (Peter, James, and John) whom Jesus trusted most implicitly. John was the only disciple present at Jesus's death on the cross. All the others had fled.

This, it seems, was Jesus's way of executing his will.

93

On the cross, Jesus was FORSAKEN by God.

"God has said, 'Never will I leave you; never will I forsake you'" (Hebrews 13:5). And yet on the cross God's only Son cried out, "My God, my God, why have you forsaken me?" (Mark 15:34). So was Jesus wrong, or had God really forsaken him? And if so, why?

Throughout his life on earth, Jesus had a perfect relationship with his Father. He prayed often and did only what his Father told him to do. He never erred and never refused to do everything the Father asked. But for one dark moment, their special fellowship was broken at the time when Jesus seemed to need his Father most. "At the sixth hour [noon] darkness came over the whole land until the ninth hour [3:00 p.m.]. And at the ninth hour Jesus cried out in a loud voice, 'Eloi, Eloi, lama sabachthani?'—which means, 'My God, my God, why have you forsaken me?'" (Mark 15:33–34). Those words are a quote from Psalm 22:1, in which David perfectly foretold the details of crucifixion (see chapter 88 on Jesus's fulfilling prophecy on the cross).

What was happening at this moment that made Jesus feel forsaken by God? Second Corinthians 5:21 gives us a clue: "God made him who had no sin to be sin for us, so that in him we might become the righteousness of God." And Isaiah 59:1–2 further completes the picture: "Surely the arm of the LORD is not too short to save, nor his ear too dull to hear. But your iniquities have separated you from your God; your sins have hidden his face from you, so that he will not hear."

The ominous darkness that covered the land—and perhaps the whole world—for those three hours presaged God the Father's separation from his Son. For a moment God's fellowship and relationship with Jesus were broken. God had forsaken his Son.

Why? In that moment, Jesus was bearing the sins of the world. He experienced complete abandonment to hell (the punishment of unforgiven sin) and, I believe, Jesus felt the spiritual agony and pain that all people throughout the ages would have experienced had they been sent to hell for their sins. Jesus endured the kind of mental and emotional pain that comes only from the deepest despair. He knew what it was to be cut off from God the Father and heaven; he knew what it was like to be in hell. Alone. Anguished. Broken. Forgotten. Destroyed. Despondent.

In that moment Jesus bore the weight of and paid the penalty for every sin of every sinner who would ever live. And in that moment he knew the agonies of the lowest hell. He experienced it all so that we might never have to experience it.

94

Jesus used a ROMAN prison term from the cross.

When Roman guards cast a criminal into prison, they nailed his sentence and conviction notice to the door of his cell. Then, when he'd completed the sentence, one word was written over the paper: "Tetelestai," meaning "It is done" or "it is finished." The criminal could then take that bit of script and show it to any who might ask about the status of his crime. "It's paid for," he could say; "it's finished."

The term was also used on tax receipts and meant "paid in full."

Jesus made seven statements from the cross, most of them discussed in this book. In John 19:28–30 we find the fifth and sixth statements he uttered: "Knowing that all was now completed, and so that the Scripture would be fulfilled, Jesus said, 'I am thirsty.' A jar of wine vinegar was there, so they soaked a sponge in it, put the sponge on a stalk of the hyssop plant, and lifted it to Jesus' lips. When he had received the drink, Jesus said, 'It is finished.' With that, he bowed his head and gave up his spirit." Mark 15:37 tells us that Jesus spoke with a loud cry. This is significant, for those who were crucified were usually too weak and had too little breath to speak at all, much less in a loud voice. But the Savior's last sounds from the cross were not a whimper of despair or a gasp for air but rather a shout of victory and triumph: "It is finished!"

Why did Jesus speak this Roman prison term from the cross? It was something every person in the crowd would have understood. The Roman soldiers especially would have known its meaning. He was saying, "I have served the sentence; paid the debt in full for every crime ever committed against humanity and God."

Jesus had completed his mission, finished the task, paid the penalty every citizen of planet Earth would otherwise have to pay. God cannot just delete sin. Justice demands that it be paid for. Hebrews 9:22 says, "In fact, the law requires that nearly everything be cleansed with blood, and without the shedding of blood there is no forgiveness." So on the cross that day, Jesus purchased our salvation and forgiveness. God the Father received justice for every human sinner. And every human sinner found a path to God through forgiveness of sins through the shed blood of Christ. All sinners must do is repent and trust in Christ.

It's the simple transaction that's the foundation of the gospel. Jesus has paid in full for our sins. We never have to pay back a single dime or drop of blood in return for our own sins. No one has to die the second death. Jesus fixed the problem and finished the sentence once and forever.

95

Jesus preached AFTER he died.

The Apostles' Creed, recited in many churches every Sunday, includes an expression that some churches use and others discard. It's found in the statement, "I believe in . . . Jesus Christ, his only Son our Lord, who was conceived by the Holy Spirit, born to the Virgin Mary, suffered under Pontius Pilate, was crucified, dead and buried; he descended into hell; the third day he rose from the dead, ascended into heaven, and sits at the right hand of God the Father."

The expression some omit and others don't is, "He descended into hell." What's this all about?

When Jesus died on the cross, his body lay in a tomb for the next three days (Friday afternoon and night, Saturday all day, and Sunday morning). Other texts in the New Testament seem to indicate that during that time the spirit of a person is alive (see Philippians 1:21–24); thus, Jesus, in his spirit, would have still been alive. So what did he do during that time?

Several passages offer some evidence. First Peter 4:6 says, "This is the reason the gospel was preached even to those who are now dead, so that they might be judged according to men in regard to the body, but live according to God in regard to the spirit." This passage seems to indicate that someone preached the gospel to the dead—all the dead from all ages up to the crucifixion and death of Christ.

First Peter does not indicate here who preached this message, but look at this earlier passage: "Christ died for sins once for all, the righteous for the unrighteous, to bring you to God. He was put to death in the body but made alive by the Spirit, through whom also he went and preached to the spirits in prison who disobeyed long ago when God waited patiently in the days of Noah while the ark was being built" (1 Peter 3:18–20).

Some interpreters believe these two passages refer to Jesus preaching to "spirits" (demons and/or dead people?) in prison (in hell?)—and telling them of his triumph over sin. This could be true, although there is much difference of opinion about this throughout church history. I personally believe from these two passages that it's possible Jesus spoke to those people and let them know that redemption had been offered—note that 1 Peter 4:6 says "gospel"—good news—not "judgment." It's possible that Jesus offered them the gift of salvation at that time, or that he simply announced what had been done. I, for one, would like to believe that God's grace is so great, Jesus might have offered those beings salvation. No one really knows for sure, and there are opposing viewpoints by faithful people on both sides of the issue.

The grander truth is that however God deals with those who have never heard the gospel or the real truth about God and Christ, God will be fair, just, and righteous in deciding their destinies. We can be sure that God is always "Compassionate and gracious, slow to anger, abounding in love and faithfulness, maintaining love to thousands, and forgiving wickedness, rebellion and sin" (Exodus 34:6–7).

96

Jesus turned fishermen into SHEPHERDS.

The disciples didn't do too well with Jesus's death on the cross. Only one actually showed up at his death, while the others fled and disappeared. After Jesus rose from the dead, he appeared to them several times, convincing them he was the Lord of life. He came to them as they gathered on several occasions, and at one point, the apostle Paul tells us, he appeared to more than five hundred disciples at the same time (see 1 Corinthians 15:3–8).

What did the disciples do in response to these momentous events? They went fishing.

John 21:1–14 tells us that seven disciples—Simon Peter, Thomas, Nathanael, James, John, and two others—fished all night, but to no avail. Only when Jesus appeared and told them where to cast their nets did they actually find any finny thing in the waters.

But doesn't the whole incident sound "fishy"? Shouldn't those disciples have been praying? Waiting in a likely place for Jesus's next appearance? Making plans for preaching the gospel to the world?

Apparently, they were so stressed by the events of Passover week and its climax on Golgotha (the hill where Jesus died on the cross) that they weren't dealing too well with anything. They needed some rest and relaxation. And what's more relaxing to a man of influence and power than a little fishing? You don't really even have to catch anything. Just get on the water, cast your line (or your net, as the case may be), and wait.

I think the disciples had reached the limits of their ability to comprehend and assimilate. They needed to do something they understood well and could perform easily. What else, other than fishing? Certainly not tax collecting or fighting with the Zealots (as Simon the Zealot might have preferred). No, just a little bait and net, and they were good to go.

Was Jesus disappointed to find them out fishing? He'd been gone such a short time. Were they slipping back into the old life now that they were on their own?

I think he understood their reaction. After all, he certainly wasn't putting them down when he gave them such a huge, miraculous catch. Perhaps he wanted to impress on them that, if fishing was what they really wanted to do for the rest of their lives, he could make it monumentally lucrative. Or maybe he just blessed them because he loved them.

But that wasn't what they really wanted. And it wasn't what he had planned for them. They had been changed forever by their association with Jesus. How could they ever go back to the way things were? They could no longer be fishermen.

"Feed my sheep," Jesus said. He had changed them from fishermen into shepherds of spiritual "sheep." He had transformed them from caring about little, daily things like fishing to having the giant purpose of changing the whole world.

In fact, that's what Jesus does with each of us when we choose to become his disciples. He opens our eyes to something bigger and grander than our own small goals and aspirations. He did that for me. The day I became a Christian, I had the distinct feeling I had suddenly become part of something bigger than graduating from high school, going to college, getting a job, getting married, and raising a family. Suddenly I wanted to be a useful servant of his in building the kingdom of God.

Isn't that what drives us? Isn't that the marvelous mission with which Jesus has captivated our souls?

So those disciples made a few detours on their journey by going fishing. But Jesus wasn't about to let them think that was all there was to the dynamic plan he had for their lives. He showed them once and for all that small ambitions are the stuff of a world that doesn't know him. For them, he had—and now has for us—something far greater.

97

Jesus DIDN'T condemn the doubter but embraced him.

Doubting Thomas, we call him. Somehow he stands alone in history. Yes, Judas Iscariot, the traitor, went to his deserved fate. And Peter, the denier, moved on from there to leadership in the early church. A few of the other disciples we know about. James was beheaded by Herod. John wrote a number of books of the New Testament but was exiled on an island called Patmos. Matthew wrote his account of Jesus, but we know little more.

And then we have Thomas. The doubter. Somehow that seems worse than the other disciples' weaknesses. But was he really alone in his doubt? And should he be singled out as some kind of failure?

Most of Thomas's story is recorded in the book of John, but of particular interest here is his role in John 20:24–31. Jesus appeared to ten of his remaining disciples when they were gathered together in a house. He also appeared to several others individually, including Peter. Thomas, for some reason, wasn't with them. Was he off mourning? Was he so devastated by Jesus's death that he just couldn't stand to be with anyone? Perhaps, but we can't know for sure.

When the disciples next saw Thomas, they told him, "We have seen the Lord!" But Thomas replied, "Unless I see the nail marks in his hands and put my finger where the nails were, and put my hand into his side, I will not believe it" (John 20:25).

Was Thomas being stubborn? Did he think his friends had gone crazy or were suffering from hallucinations or something worse? We don't know. But from Thomas's statement, it seems that just seeing Jesus would not be enough for him. He had to be sure Jesus was more than an illusion, more than a ghost. If Jesus had risen in physical form, then to confirm this, Thomas wanted to touch him, to feel the cruel marks of his death; to be utterly, truly, completely, and forever sure of the truth so he could believe.

Was he alone in this?

Actually, all the disciples doubted. Only John made it to the crucifixion. Peter was out weeping over his denials. The others had fled in fear for their lives. None of them truly believed Jesus would be resurrected, even though he had told them numerous times that it would happen.

In Luke 24:36–43 we read that the disciples were having their own hard time believing the report two of Jesus's followers had brought them about their encounter with the risen Christ on the road to Emmaus. They told how Jesus had walked with them, talked with them, and explained from Scripture what had been happening, but that they hadn't recognized it was Jesus until he broke bread with them. Suddenly Jesus himself was among them and greeted them, "Peace be with you" (Luke 24:36). Unlike Thomas the doubter, these guys immediately recognized and embraced Jesus, right? Wrong!

"They were startled and frightened, thinking they saw a ghost. He said to them, 'Why are you troubled, and why do doubts rise in your minds? Look at my hands and my feet. It is I myself! Touch me and see; a ghost does not have flesh and bones, as you see I have'" (Luke 24:37–39). Wouldn't you want to know on that level? Just seeing Jesus wasn't enough. Later Jesus even ate some fish to prove he was real and alive.

It seems all of Jesus's followers were afflicted with this unbelief. It's just that Thomas hadn't experienced the risen Jesus, and that was what he wanted, what he needed.

So Jesus appeared to them all again. And he didn't waste words or beat around the bush. Somehow he knew what Thomas had said; he knew what Thomas needed. He immediately turned to the last doubting holdout and said, "Put your finger here; see my hands. Reach out your hand and put it into my side. Stop doubting and believe" (John 20:27).

That was enough for Thomas. He didn't hesitate but worshiped Christ in that moment, crying out, "My Lord and my God!" (John 20:28). This is a most powerful exclamation of faith and affirmation of Jesus's deity, and a rare instance in the Gospels where someone called Jesus his God.

Next Jesus gave a word of promise and affirmation to all who would ever believe: "Because you have seen me, you have believed; blessed are those who have not seen and yet have believed" (John 20:29).

What a tremendous word of joy. We do not have the luxury of Thomas and the disciples and those early Christians to actually see and touch Jesus; but because they were hard to convince, because they required physical proof, it helps sincere doubters today to find faith. And somehow, because of the work of the Spirit in us, the persuasiveness of the Gospels, and the simple statements of those who have believed before us, we also have come to this place. And guess what? One day we will see Jesus glorified, in the flesh, and he will be with us forever.

Thomas, I'm looking forward to meeting you.

98

Jesus lives IN our hearts.

"To all who received him, to those who believed in his name, he gave the right to become children of God" (John 1:12). This just may be the most frequently quoted passage in the Bible for "receiving Jesus into your heart" and becoming a child of God.

Some base the teaching on Revelation 3:20, where Jesus said to the errant church at Laodicea, "Here I am! I stand at the door [of your heart] and knock. If anyone hears my voice and opens the door, I will come in and eat with him, and he with me."

From these two passages we might get the idea that Jesus comes into our hearts and somehow lives there. But the New Testament is clear on the identity of this indwelling person. He's not Jesus; he's the Holy Spirit. For instance, consider 1 Corinthians 6:19–20: "Do you not know that your body is the temple of the Holy Spirit, who is in you, whom you have received from God? You are not your own; you were bought at a price. Therefore honor God with your body." We find this idea of the Spirit dwelling in us in many places in the Bible, and the heart is his dwelling place—though not the physical heart but rather the heart as seat of the emotions, mind, and will, which in the Jewish theology was the center of the self.

So does Jesus ever dwell there? Yes! According to John 14:23 Jesus told his disciples in his great discourse in the upper room, where he shared his last meal with them, "If anyone loves me he will obey my teaching. My Father will love him, and we will come to him and make our home with him." This is a clear echo of John 1:12 and Revelation 3:20. In some supernatural sense, according to this passage, all three members of the Trinity make their home or live and dwell within believers.

Thus, the imagery of Jesus living in our hearts isn't such a bad one after all.

99

Jesus PREPARED believers for his Second Coming.

One of the things the disciples most wanted to know about was when Jesus would return. This was not because they understood that he had to die on the cross but because he kept telling them he would soon die and rise three days later. It must have finally started sinking in, because as Jesus neared the end, his disciples asked him, "When will this happen, and what will be the sign of your coming and of the end of the age?" (Matthew 24:3).

Jesus warned them not to be deceived by anyone claiming to be the Messiah or Christ. Then he told them about some things that would happen before his Second Coming.

False messiahs: Many people will come in Jesus's name, saying, "I am the Christ" (see Matthew 24:4–5). Many will be deceived into thinking these people really are him.

War: Jesus said, "You will hear of wars and rumors of wars, but see to it that you are not alarmed. Such things must happen, but the end is still to come. Nation will rise against nation, and kingdom against kingdom" (Matthew 24:6–7).

Famine and earthquakes: Jesus said, "There will be famines and earthquakes in various places" (Matthew 24:7). But he likened such terrible events to merely the beginning of birth pains.

Persecution: Followers of the true Christ "will be handed over to be persecuted and put to death, and you will be hated by all nations because of me" (Matthew 24:9).

Apostasy: Many will turn away from the faith and will "betray and hate each other" (Matthew 24:10).

Religious deception: Jesus warned his followers, "Many false prophets will appear and deceive many people" (Matthew 24:11).

Moral decline: Jesus said that in the last days, wickedness—lawlessness, hatred, sin, and immorality—would increase (see Matthew 24:10–12).

Lovelessness: "The love of most will grow cold" (Matthew 24:12). People will become incapable of showing real love and will become utterly self-centered and out for themselves.

Spread of the gospel: Jesus said, "This gospel of the kingdom will be preached in the whole world as a testimony to all nations, and then the end will come" (Matthew 24:14). Every group will be reached and will hear the good news about Jesus.

"Abomination that causes desolation": This is a term Jesus's Jewish listeners would have recognized from the book of Daniel (8:13; 9:27; 11:31; 12:11). It relates in part to Antiochus Epiphanes sacrificing a pig on the temple altar in 168 BC, but it also appears this was a picture of something yet to come, relating to the Antichrist who will appear in the Last Days.

False signs and miracles: Jesus told the disciples, "False Christs and false prophets will appear and perform great signs and miracles to deceive even the elect—if that were possible. See, I have told you ahead of time" Matthew 24:24–25).

Signs in the heavens: "Immediately after the distress of those days 'the sun will be darkened, and the moon will not give its light; the stars will fall from the sky, and the heavenly bodies will be shaken'" (Matthew 24:29). (Jesus was quoting from Isaiah 13:10 and 34:4.)

All these things would precede the return of Christ. Then, "At that time the sign of the Son of Man will appear in the sky, and all the nations of the earth will mourn. They will see the Son of Man coming on the clouds of the sky, with power and great glory. And he will send his angels with a loud trumpet call, and they will gather his elect from the four winds, from one end of the heavens to the other" (Matthew 24:30–31).

So when will these things occur? Jesus summed it all up with the words, "No one knows about that day or hour, not even the angels in heaven, nor the Son, but only the Father" (Matthew 24:36).

What should we do in light of this prophecy? Jesus has two words of advice: "Keep watch" (Matthew 24:42).

100

Jesus has made SURE
we get there.

One of the greatest things about being a Christian is the security we have in Jesus. We might worry that something could mess up our salvation, or we might do something so heinous that God would turn away from us. We might fear God will somehow change his mind about us and send us off to hell just for the fun of it.

But we don't have to worry about such things. Consider the great promise of Jesus when the Jews asked him, "How long will you keep us in suspense? If you are the Christ, tell us plainly" (John 10:24). For once, the leaders of the Jews seemed completely open, wanting to know if Jesus really was who others said he was and who he had hinted he was all along. But watch what happened at the end of this little exchange:

Jesus answered their question by saying, "I did tell you, but you do not believe. The miracles I do in my Father's name speak for me, but you do not believe because you are not my sheep. My sheep listen to my voice; I know them, and they follow me. I give them eternal life, and they shall never perish; no one can snatch them out of my hand. My Father, who has given them to me, is greater than all; no one can snatch them out of my Father's hand. I and the Father are one" (John 10:25–30).

Notice that Jesus pointed to the one verifiable thing these people could see that proved he was the Messiah: his miracles. They spoke for him.

However, he said the reason they didn't believe was because they were not his sheep. He meant they had rejected Christ all along, so they weren't selected by God to be his disciples, followers, and servants.

But then, in John 10:27–28, Jesus made an incredible promise to his own followers. Let's break it down:

1. "My sheep listen to my voice." Make no mistake about it; if you belong to Jesus, one day you will hear him speak to your heart, and you will know it's him.

2. "I know them." To personally know God is to be at one with him and to be his child.

3. "They follow me." Those who hear Christ's voice follow. They don't give up. They don't get lost. They don't change paths to follow a new religion or a new path. They stick to Jesus.

4. "I give them eternal life." He gives all his sheep both a quality (fulfilling, joyous, enlarging, transforming) of life and a quantity (eternal) of life.

5. "They shall never perish." They shall never die the second death, cease to exist, or be forgotten.

6. "No one can snatch them out of my hand." Not the devil, not Rome, not a persuasive atheist, not an unbelieving professor—no one—can strip this person of his salvation and take him away from God.

Incredible. Wouldn't everyone want that for themselves?

After all this, Jesus answered the Jews' question: "I and the Father are one." Jesus and his Father are equals, both divine, both everlasting, both all-powerful.

The Jews had asked Jesus to tell them who he was. That's exactly what he'd done. What did they do in response? "Again the Jews picked up stones to stone him" (John 10:31).

So Jesus said, "I have shown you many great miracles from the Father. For which of these do you stone me?" (John 10:32).

"We are not stoning you for any of these," replied the Jews, "but for blasphemy, because you, a mere man, claim to be God" (John 10:33).

It was a Catch-22. If Jesus didn't reveal his identity, they would keep hounding him. And when he did reveal it, they wanted to stone him.

But the great truth is that none of Jesus's real sheep would turn on him like this. They hear his voice, are forever changed, and follow him through all eternity.

101

Jesus will come back to the
MOUNT OF OLIVES.

There is some confusion about precisely how Jesus will come back to earth. The concept of the Second Coming is based on three passages of the New Testament.

The first is Matthew 24:27–31, where Jesus told the disciples:

> As lightning that comes from the east is visible even in the west, so will be the coming of the Son of Man. Wherever there is a carcass, there the vultures will gather.
>
> Immediately after the distress of those days "the sun will be darkened, and the moon will not give its light; the stars will fall from the sky, and the heavenly bodies will be shaken."
>
> At that time the sign of the Son of Man will appear in the sky, and all the nations of the earth will mourn. They will see the Son of Man coming on the clouds of the sky, with power and great glory. And he will send his angels with a loud trumpet call, and they will gather his elect from the four winds, from one end of the heavens to the other.

Clearly, Jesus's coming will be marked by miracles. He will appear in the sky and come down accompanied by angels.

The second passage, Acts 1:10–11, includes the words of an angel at Jesus's ascension: "They [the disciples] were looking intently up into the sky as he was going, when suddenly two men dressed in white stood beside them. 'Men of Galilee,' they said, 'why do you stand here looking into the sky? This same Jesus, who has been taken from you into heaven, will come back in the same way you have seen him go into heaven.'"

From this we can surmise it will be something like the ascension, Jesus's rising up into the clouds to heaven, except in reverse. He will come to the same location as he was when he left: the Mount of Olives (which still exists in Jerusalem today).

Finally, the revelation of Christ's return as shown to John the apostle, in Revelation 19:11–16. John wrote:

> I saw heaven standing open and there before me was a white horse, whose rider is called Faithful and True. With justice he judges and makes war. His eyes are like blazing fire, and on his head are many crowns. He has a name written on him that no one knows but he himself. He is dressed in a robe dipped in blood, and his name is the Word of God. The armies of heaven were following him, riding on white horses and dressed in fine linen, white and clean. Out of his mouth comes a sharp sword with which to strike down the nations. "He will rule them with an iron scepter" [a quote from Psalm 2:9]. He treads the winepress of the fury of the wrath of God Almighty. On his robe and on his thigh he has this name written: KING OF KINGS AND LORD OF LORDS.

In this passage we see Jesus on a white horse with the armies of heaven moving toward us from the heavens.

One other passage, from the Old Testament, is also important. Zechariah 14:4 says, "On that day his feet will stand on the Mount of Olives, east of Jerusalem, and the Mount of Olives will be split in two from east to west, forming a great valley, with half of the mountain moving north and half moving south." From the context we know this refers to Jesus's Second Coming.

Which passage is correct?

All four are. How, then, will Jesus return?

In the sky with clouds.

Riding on a white horse.

With the armies of heaven.

To the Mount of Olives.

Be watching. It *will* happen, perhaps in our lifetime.